A SPECIAL GIFT

❧ ❧ ❧

Presented to

_____

From

_____

Date

_____

A RAINBOW OF HOPE

777 Inspirational Quotes **PLUS** *Selected Scriptures*

FOREWORD

❧ ❧ ❧

RAINBOW STUDIES, INC. publishes *A Rainbow of Hope* as well as THE RAINBOW STUDY BIBLE, which introduced the color-code study system that changed Bible reading for hundreds of thousands! THE RAINBOW STUDY BIBLE color-codes every verse of Scripture in one of 12 colors, each representing one of 12 major themes. GREEN verses are about LOVE; ORANGE–FAITH; BLUE–SALVATION; etc. This allows the reader to find verses most applicable to individual needs easily and efficiently.

Now, with this beautifully illustrated inspirational book, *A Rainbow of Hope*, you can apply this system not only to the book of *PROVERBS* at the back, but also to the quotes of many famous and interesting people. Wait till you hear what Will Rogers and Dwight D. Eisenhower have to say about *WAR*. It's all in the SILVER *HISTORY* chapter. Abraham Lincoln not only practiced *PRAYER*, but he had something to say about it. So does Dale Evans Rogers. It's all in the ORANGE *FAITH* chapter.

A Rainbow of Hope, with its color-code system, makes finding true nuggets of wisdom as easy as a kindergartner learning his colors. You'll enjoy the RAINBOW color-code study system!

—The Publisher

Color Coded Guide for Subject Headings

❧ ❧ ❧

TABLE OF CONTENTS

TABLE OF CONTENTS

❦ ❦ ❦

God

CHAPTER ONE

DESCRIBE GOD

✻ ✻ ✻

*I*mpossible! Because God is so much more than attributes such as "love" and "light." God is a personality with specific likes and dislikes. I am convinced that one of God's greatest enjoyments is in His COLORS.

This fact is confirmed in the world He spoke into existence with sparkling blue rivers, luscious green forests, rich brown soil, and the orange and reds of an evening at sunset. God's love for colors is further validated by scripture which states that a rainbow encircles the very throne of God (Revelation 4:3).

Oh, how He must enjoy COLORS! Have you learned to enjoy all colors as God does? Have you learned those things that God likes and dislikes?

Red and Yellow, Black and White,
They are all precious in His sight.

People
SEE GOD
every day,
THEY just DON'T
RECOGNIZE
him.

Pearl Bailey

God

Be still, and know that I am God....
Psalm 46:10 NIV

Who else but God goes back and forth to heaven?
Who else holds the wind in his fists
and wraps up the oceans in his cloak?
Who but God has created the world?
If there is any other, what is his name—
and his Son's name—if you know it?
Proverbs 30:4 TLB

If God be for us, who can be against us?
Romans 8:31 KJV

But you may not see the glory of my face,
for man may not see me and live.
Exodus 33:20 TLB

God is spirit....

John 4:24 NIV

❧

God is one.

Galatians 3:20 NIV

❧

God is light....

1 John 1:5 NIV

❧

God is love.

1 John 4:8 NIV

*G*reat bursts of light flashed forth from him..:
and a rainbow glowing like an emerald
encircled his throne.

Revelation 4:3 TLB

❧

*G*od cannot be solemn, or he would not have
blessed man with the incalculable gift of laughter.

Sydney Harris

❧

*G*od warms his hands at man's heart when he prays.

John Masefield

❧

Light is the shadow of God.

Plato

❧

*G*od often visits us,
but most of the time we are not at home.

French Proverb

❧

*T*here is comfort in the fact that God
can never be taken by surprise.

Gabelein

*N*o one can study chemistry and see
the wonderful way in which certain elements
combine with the nicety of the most delicate
machine ever invented, and not come
to the inevitable conclusion that there is a
Big Engineer who is running this universe.

Thomas Edison

*W*hen you have nothing left but God,
then for the first time you
become aware that God is enough.

Maude Royden

*W*hat does it mean to have a god, or,
what is God?... your god in reality
is that around which you entwine your heart
and on which you place your confidence.

Martin Luther

God Almighty does not throw dice.

Albert Einstein

the Father

*K*now then in your heart that as a man
disciplines his son,
so the LORD your God disciplines you.
Deuteronomy 8:5 NIV

*A*s a father has compassion on his children,
so the LORD has compassion
on those who fear him....
Psalm 103:13 NIV

the Son, Jesus Christ

For unto us a child is born,
unto us a son is given:
and the government
shall be upon his shoulder:
and his name shall be called
Wonderful, Counsellor,
The mighty God,
The everlasting Father,
The Prince of Peace.

Isaiah 9:6 KJV

For even the Son of Man
did not come to be served, but to serve,
and to give his life as a ransom for many.

Mark 10:45 NIV

Jesus Christ is the same
yesterday, today, and forever.

Hebrews 13:8 TLB

I am the bread of life....

John 6:35 KJV

❧

I am the light of the world....

John 8:12 KJV

❧

I am the door....

John 10:9 KJV

❧

I am the good shepherd....

John 10:11 KJV

❧

I am the resurrection, and the life....

John 11:25 KJV

❧

I am the way, the truth, and the life....

John 14:6 KJV

❧

I AM the true vine....

John 15:1 KJV

*J*esus! it is the name
which moves the harps of heaven to melody...
a gathering up of the hallelujahs of eternity
in five letters.

Charles Spurgeon

⁂

*I*n his life, Christ is an example,
showing us how to live;
in his death, he is a sacrifice,
satisfying for our sins;
in his resurrection, a conqueror;
in his ascension, a king;
in his intercession, a high priest.

Martin Luther

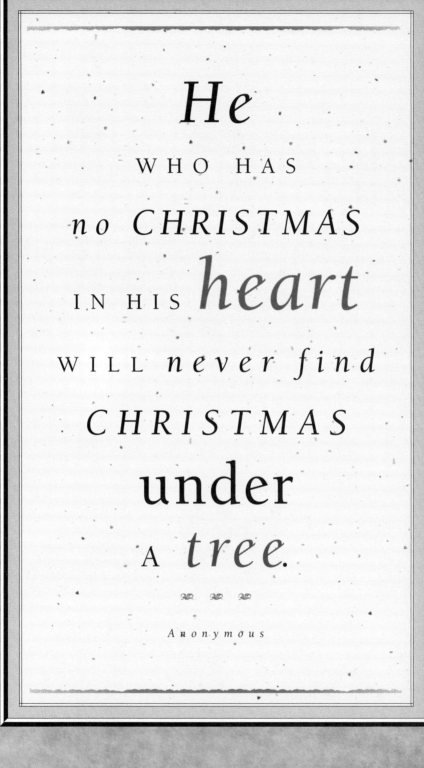

He
WHO HAS
no CHRISTMAS
IN HIS *heart*
WILL *never find*
CHRISTMAS
under
A *tree.*

Anonymous

the Holy Spirit

*N*ot by might,
nor by power,
but by my Spirit,
says the Lord Almighty....
Zechariah 4:6 TLB

*D*on't you know that you yourselves
are God's temple
and that God's Spirit lives in you?
1 Corinthians 3:16 NIV

*C*loser is He than breathing,
and nearer than hands and feet.
Alfred, Lord Tennyson

the Word of God

For the word of God is quick, and powerful,
and sharper than any two-edged sword....
Hebrews 4:12 KJV

And the words of the LORD are
flawless,
like silver refined in a furnace of
clay,
purified seven times.
Psalm 12:6 NIV

Heaven and earth will pass away,
but my words will never pass away.
Matthew 24:35 NIV

God's laws are pure, eternal, just.
They are more desirable than gold.
They are sweeter than honey
dripping from a honeycomb.
For they warn us away from harm
and give success to those who obey them.
Psalm 19:9-11 TLB

Thy word is a lamp unto my feet,
and a light unto my path.
Psalm 119:105 KJV

The grass withers,
the flowers fade,
but the Word of our God
shall stand forever.
Isaiah 40:8 TLB

The whole Bible was given to us
by inspiration from God
and is useful to teach us
what is true and to make us realize
what is wrong in our lives;
it straightens us out and helps us
do what is right.
2 Timothy 3:16 TLB

The first and almost the only Book
deserving of universal attention is the Bible.
John Quincy Adams

*D*o you know a book that you
are willing to put under your head
for a pillow when you lie dying?
That is the book you want to study
while you are living.
There is but one such book in the world.
The Bible.

Joseph Cook

❧

*T*his Book will keep you from sin,
or sin will keep you from this Book.

D. L. Moody

❧

A thorough knowledge of the Bible
is worth more than a college education.

Theodore Roosevelt

❧

*W*ithin the covers of this single book
are all the answers to all the problems
that face us today, if we would only look there.

Ronald Reagan

*I know the Bible is inspired
because it inspires me.*
D. L. Moody

❦

*I*t is impossible to rightly govern the world
without God and the Bible.
George Washington

❦

*N*obody ever outgrows Scripture;
the book widens and deepens with our years.
Charles Spurgeon

❦

"*W*hat parable in the Bible do you like best?"
was the question asked of a little boy.
And the answer was,
"The one about the fellow that loafs and fishes."
Anonymous

There IS A
Book
WORTH all
other BOOKS
which WERE
ever
printed.

❧ ❧ ❧

Patrick Henry

G O D

Savior

I, even I, am the LORD,
and apart from me there is no
savior.

Isaiah 43:11 NIV

ЖЕ   ЖЕ   ЖЕ

*G*od pardons like a mother
who kisses away the repentant tears
of her child.

Henry Ward Beecher

The LORD does not look at the things man
looks at. Man looks at the outward appearance,
but the LORD looks at the heart.

1 Samuel 16:7 NIV

O Lord, you have examined my heart
and know everything about me.
You know when I sit or stand....
You know what I am going to say
before I even say it.

Psalm 139:1-4 TLB

For my thoughts are not your thoughts,
neither are your ways my ways, saith the LORD.

Isaiah 55:8 KJV

*T*he LORD is gracious and compassionate,
slow to anger and rich in love.
Psalm 145:8 NIV

*W*ith the Lord a day is like a thousand years,
and a thousand years are like a day.
2 Peter 3:8 NIV

O LORD, our Lord,
how majestic is your name in all the earth!
Psalm 8:1 NIV

Messiah

*T*hen Jesus told her, "I am the Messiah!"
John 4:26 TLB

I AM

*A*nd God said unto Moses, I AM THAT I AM....

Exodus 3:14 KJV

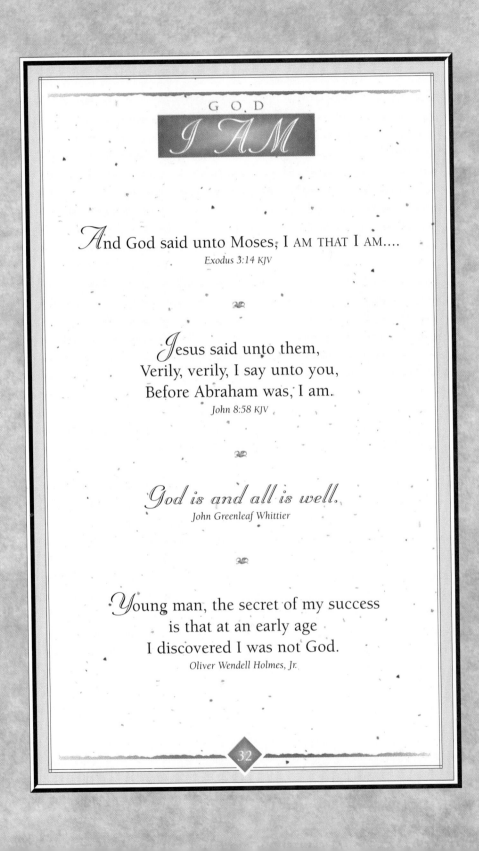

*J*esus said unto them,
Verily, verily, I say unto you,
Before Abraham was, I am.

John 8:58 KJV

God is and all is well.

John Greenleaf Whittier

*Y*oung man, the secret of my success
is that at an early age
I discovered I was not God.

Oliver Wendell Holmes, Jr.

Lamb of God

He was led like a lamb to the
slaughter,
and as a sheep before her shearers is
silent,
so he did not open his mouth.

Isaiah 53:7 NIV

The next day John saw Jesus
coming toward him and said,
"Look, the Lamb of God,
who takes away the sin of the world!"

John 1:29 NIV

G O D

King of Kings

*H*ow awesome is the LORD Most High,
the great King over all the earth!

Psalm 47:2 NIV

🙢 🙢 🙢

*J*esus answered,
"You are right in saying I am a king.
In fact, for this reason I was born,
and for this I came into the world...."

John 18:37 NIV

Alpha & Omega

I am the Alpha and the Omega,
the First and the Last,
the Beginning and the End.
Revelation 22:13 NIV

God is patient because eternal.
St. Augustine

*G*od is a circle whose center is everywhere
and whose circumference is nowhere.
Empedocles

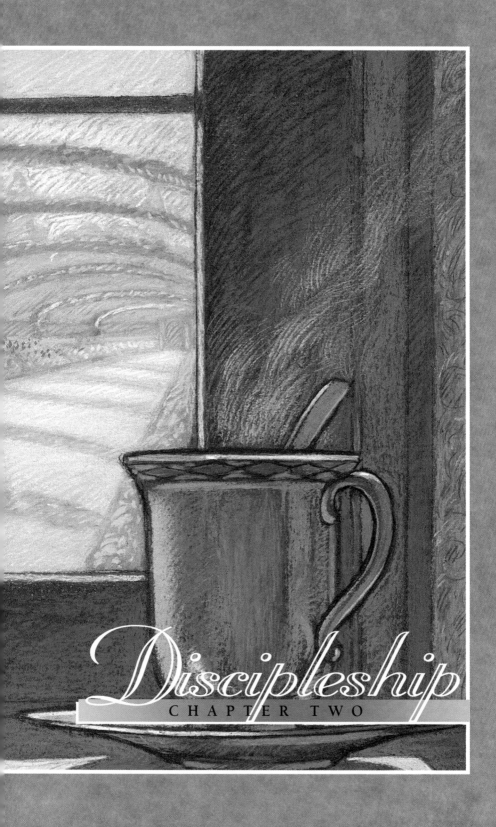

Discipleship

CHAPTER TWO

BE A DISCIPLE

❧ ❧ ❧

*H*igh school and college years are demanding. Young people are making decisions regarding careers and future goals that are life-changing. Ask anyone who has suffered through dissecting frogs in biology or running laps in gym class, and he'll quickly let you know that you will love it immensely or hate it intensely!

Getting down to the nitty-gritty changes things. Questions have to be asked: *Do I believe in what I'm doing? Do I even like it?* The answers may be crucial, for years of one's life may be spent in that field.

Following God requires that same planning and commitment. If we truly believe that God has a plan for our lives, then we should follow Him wholeheartedly and serve Him fully.

We focus our time and talents on those things that are important to us. *Making a living* is important, but *living for the Maker* is most important!

Be His disciple.

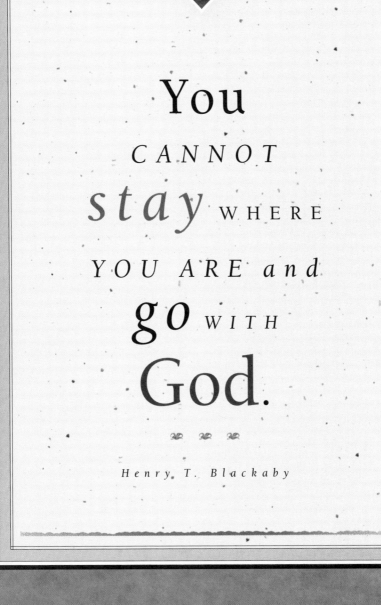

You
CANNOT
stay WHERE
YOU ARE *and*
go WITH
God.

❧ ❧ ❧

Henry T. Blackaby

Discipleship

*A*nd no one can be my disciple
who does not carry his own cross and follow me.
Luke 14:27 TLB

❧

*Don't bother to give God instructions;
just report for duty.*
Corrie ten Boom

❧

*C*hristianity is called a spiritual walk.
It's not a run and it's not a jog.
It's a walk you do from day to day
and that makes you stable.
Orel Hershiser

❧

*I*f you live for the next world,
you get this one in the deal;
but if you live only for this world,
you lose them both.
C. S. Lewis

Do not have your concert first
and tune your instruments afterward.
Begin the day with God.
J. Hudson Taylor

※

What we do during our working hours
determines what we have;
what we do in our leisure hours
determines what we are.
George Eastman

※

Character may be manifested
in the great moments,
but it is made in the small ones.
Phillips Brooks

※

Character is what you
are in the dark.
D. L. Moody

Christ is not valued at all
unless he is valued above all.

St. Augustine

My life is devoted to Christ.
It is for him that I breathe and see.
I can't bear the pain when people
call me a social worker.
Had I been in social work,
I would have left it long ago.

Mother Teresa

No pain, no palm;
no thorns, no throne;
no gall, no glory;
no cross, no crown.

William Penn

Obedience

Here is my final conclusion:
fear God and obey his commandments,
for this is the entire duty of man.

Ecclesiastes 12:13 TLB

To have a right to do a thing
is not at all the same as to be right in doing it.

G. K. Chesterton

God hasn't called me to be successful.
He's called me to be faithful.

Mother Teresa

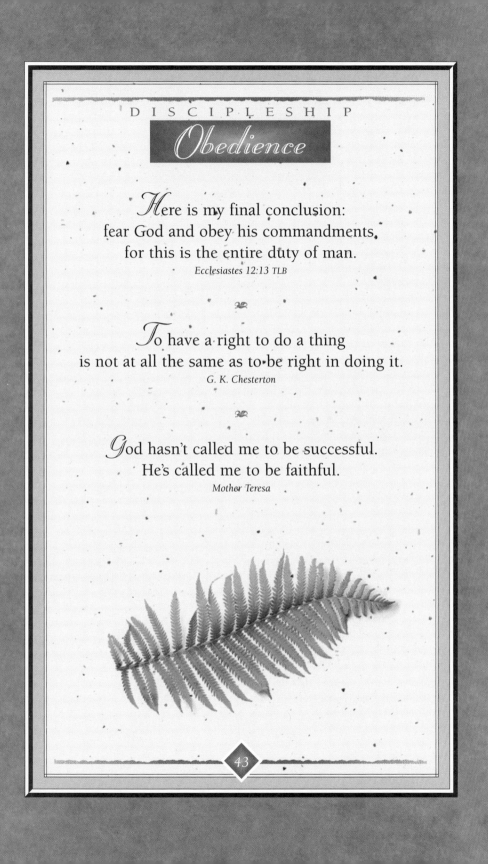

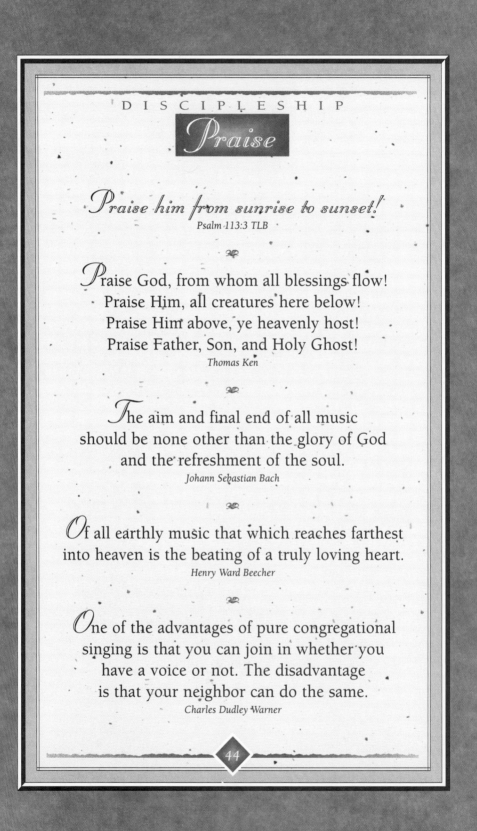

Praise

Praise him from sunrise to sunset!
Psalm 113:3 TLB

❧

Praise God, from whom all blessings flow!
Praise Him, all creatures here below!
Praise Him above, ye heavenly host!
Praise Father, Son, and Holy Ghost!

Thomas Ken

❧

The aim and final end of all music
should be none other than the glory of God
and the refreshment of the soul.

Johann Sebastian Bach

❧

Of all earthly music that which reaches farthest
into heaven is the beating of a truly loving heart.

Henry Ward Beecher

❧

One of the advantages of pure congregational
singing is that you can join in whether you
have a voice or not. The disadvantage
is that your neighbor can do the same.

Charles Dudley Warner

Service

*W*hoever serves me must follow me;
and where I'am,
my servant also will be.
My Father will honor the one
who serves me.

John 12:26 NIV

*F*ull grown oaks are not produced in three years;
neither are servants of God.

Douglas Rumford

I see Jesus in every human being.
I say to myself, this is hungry Jesus,
I must feed him. This is sick Jesus.
This one has leprosy or gangrene;
I must wash him and tend to him.
I serve because I love Jesus.

Mother Teresa

*L*et us, then, be up and doing,
With a heart for any fate;
Still achieving, still pursuing,
Learn to labor and to wait.

Henry Wadsworth Longfellow

*N*o one is useless in this world
who lightens the burdens of another.
Charles Dickens

❧

*T*o serve is beautiful, but only if it is done with joy
and a whole heart and a free mind.
Pearl S. Buck

❧

Well done is better than well said.
Benjamin Franklin

❧

A good many are kept out of the service of Christ,
deprived of the luxury of working for God,
because they are trying to do some great thing.
Let us be willing to do little things. And let us
remember that nothing is small in which God is.
D. L. Moody

❧

*D*o all the good you can,
By all the means you can,
In all the ways you can,
In all the places you can,
At all the times you can,
To all the people you can,
As long as you ever can.
John Wesley

Worship

O come, let us worship and bow down:
let us kneel before the LORD our maker.
Psalm 95:6 KJV

❧

*W*hen you recognize God as Creator,
you will admire him.
When you recognize his wisdom,
you will learn from him.
When you discover his strength,
you will rely on him.
But only when he saves you
will you worship him.
Max Lucado

❧

*I fear God, and next to God
I chiefly fear him who fears him not.*
Saadi

For wisdom is better than rubies;
and all the things that may be desired
are not to be compared to it.
Proverbs 8:11 KJV

❧

We can be knowledgeable
with other men's knowledge,
but we cannot be wise with
other men's wisdom.
Michel de Montaigne

❧

*K*nowledge is proud
that he has learn'd so much;
Wisdom is humble
that he knows no more.
William Cowper

To know the will of God
is the highest of all wisdom.
Billy Graham

❧

Wisdom is the quality that keeps you
from getting into situations where you need it.
Doug Larson

❧

*A fool may have his coat embroidered with gold,
but it is a fool's coat still.*
Antoine Rivarol

❧

That which the fool does in the end
the wise man does in the beginning.
R. C. Trench

Learning sleeps and snores in libraries,
but wisdom is everywhere,
wide awake, on tiptoe.

Josh Billings

❧

Common sense in an uncommon degree
is what the world calls wisdom.

Samuel Taylor Coleridge

❧

A man begins cutting his wisdom teeth
the first time he bites off more than he can chew.

Herb Caen

❧

Intelligence is when you spot the flaw
in your boss's reasoning.
Wisdom is when you
refrain from pointing it out.

James Dent

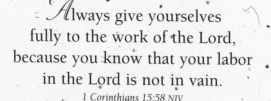

Works

*A*lways give yourselves
fully to the work of the Lord,
because you know that your labor
in the Lord is not in vain.

1 Corinthians 15:58 NIV

*M*onuments! what are they?
the very pyramids have forgotten their builders,
or to whom they were dedicated.
Deeds, not stones, are the true monuments
of the great.

John L. Motley

I am only one; but still I am one.
I cannot do everything,
but still I can do something;
I will not refuse to do the something
I can do.

Helen Keller

When your work speaks for itself,
don't interrupt.
Henry J. Kaiser

❧

*S*triving for success without hard work
is like trying to harvest
where you haven't planted.
David Bly

❧

*O*ur deeds determine us,
as much as we determine our deeds.
George Eliot

❧

*S*uccess comes before work
only in the dictionary.
Anonymous

That we are alive today
is proof positive that God
has something for us to do today.

Lindsay

I long to accomplish great and noble tasks,
but it is my chief duty and joy
to accomplish humble tasks
as though they were great and noble.

Helen Keller

To think too long about doing a thing
often becomes its undoing.

Eva Young

Don't let what you cannot do
interfere with what you can do.
John Wooden

❧

If you have built castles in the air,
your work need not be lost;
that is where they should be.
Now put foundations under them.
Henry David Thoreau

❧

The beginning is the most important part
of the work.
Plato

Never be lacking in zeal,
but keep your spiritual fervor,
serving the Lord.
Romans 12:11 NIV

In this old world of give and take
there aren't many willing to give all it takes.
Anonymous

If opportunity doesn't knock, build a door.
Milton Berle

In the second grade,
they asked us what we wanted to be.
I said I wanted to be a ballplayer
and they laughed. In the eighth grade,
they asked us the same question.
I said, "A ballplayer,"
and they laughed a little more.
By the eleventh grade,
no one was laughing.
Johnny Bench

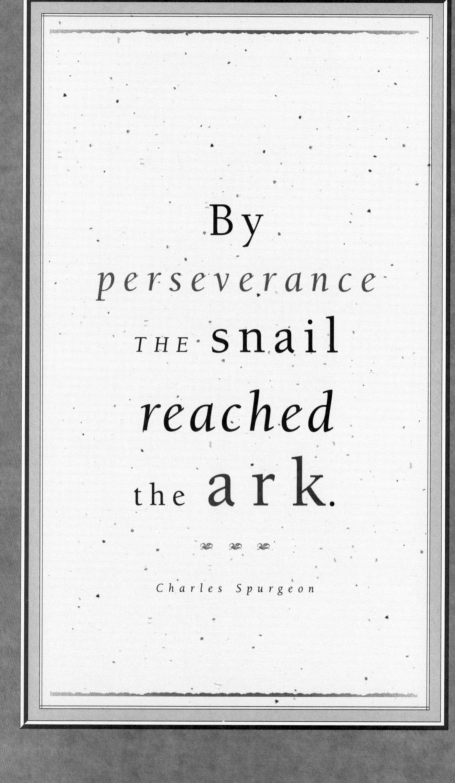

By
perseverance
THE snail
reached
the ark.

Charles Spurgeon

*W*hat matters is not the size of the dog
in the fight,
but the size of the fight
in the dog.
Dwight D. Eisenhower

*S*uccess seems to be largely a matter
of hanging on after others have let go.
William Feather

*T*he man who wins
may have been counted out several times,
but he didn't hear the referee.
H. E. Jansen

*T*he will to win is not nearly as important
as the will to prepare to win.
Bobby Knight

❧

Fall seven times, stand up eight.
Japanese Proverb

❧

*T*he way I see it, if you want the rainbow,
you gotta put up with the rain.
Dolly Parton

❧

*T*he man who removes a mountain
begins by carrying away small stones.
Chinese Proverb

When the going gets tough,
the tough get going.

Knute Rockne

❧

Genius,
that power which dazzles mortal eyes,
Is often perseverance in disguise.

Henry Willard Austin

Fellowship

*B*ut if we are living in the light
of God's presence, just as Christ does,
then we have wonderful fellowship
and joy with each other....

1 John 1:7 TLB

*N*o man is an island," said poet John Donne.
I believe every man is an island,
but there are no limits to the bridges
or harbors one can build.

Roy C. Cook

*W*henever two people meet
there are really six people present.
There is each man as he sees himself,
each man as the other person sees him,
and each man as he really is.

William James

Jesus called out to them,
"Come, follow me!
And I will make you fishermen
for the souls of men!"
At once they left their nets
and went along with him.

Mark 1:17-18 TLB

The strength of a man
consists in finding out
the way God is going,
and going that way.

Henry Ward Beecher

To know the will of God
is the greatest knowledge,
to find the will of God
is the greatest discovery,
and to do the will of God
is the greatest achievement.

George W. Truett

The great thing in this world
is not so much where we are,
but in what direction we are moving.
Oliver Wendell Holmes, Sr.

❧

Two men please God—who serves Him
with all his heart because he knows Him;
who seeks Him with all his heart
because he knows Him not.
Nikita Panin

❧

No man ever got lost on a straight road.
Abraham Lincoln

❧

Even if you are on the right track,
you'll get run over if you just sit there.
Will Rogers

Spiritual Gifts

*S*ince you are eager to have spiritual gifts,
try to excel in gifts that build up the church.

1 Corinthians 14:12 NIV

*G*od made you as you are
in order to use you as he planned.

S. C. McAuley

God's
GIFTS PUT
man's best
DREAMS
to shame.

⁂

Elizabeth Barrett Browning

This is to my Father's glory,
that you bear much fruit,
showing yourselves to be my disciples.

John 15:8 NIV

Good thoughts bear good fruit,
bad thoughts bear bad fruit—
and man is his own gardener.

James Allen

Work implies effort and labor:
the essential idea of fruit
is that it is the silent natural
restful produce of our inner life.

Andrew Murray

Love

CHAPTER THREE

PLEASE LOVE ME

≈≈ ≈≈ ≈≈

Our fifth-grade class had just gotten home from our day at the zoo. It had been such a perfect day, and I was in love. Some years later I was informed that such love is "only" puppy love. But, hey, it's real to the puppy.

The bus trip to the zoo in the city was more excitement than a country boy like me could take. We held hands most of the way. I even got the nerve to put my arm around her shoulder once, but the other guys started teasing. Later she and her best friend sang their own version of the song "Johnny Angel" to me, but with my name inserted in place of Johnny's.

But now the telephone was ringing. My perfect day was ending with these devastating words: "I no longer love you. Tommy is my boyfriend now."

Unrequited love. Oh, what a hurt! One that I experienced two or three more times through the years. But how comforting to learn that when we love without being loved back, we are at least in one small way better able to understand the heart of God.

Isn't that exactly what God experiences every day. He loves us so completely that He sent His Son to die for our sins. The pain He must feel when we do not love Him in return. But regardless of our feelings for Him, each of us can confidently proclaim:

"Just as I am, God loves me."

TO
love
IS TO make
OF ONE'S heart
A *swinging*
door.

❧ ❧ ❧

Howard Thurman

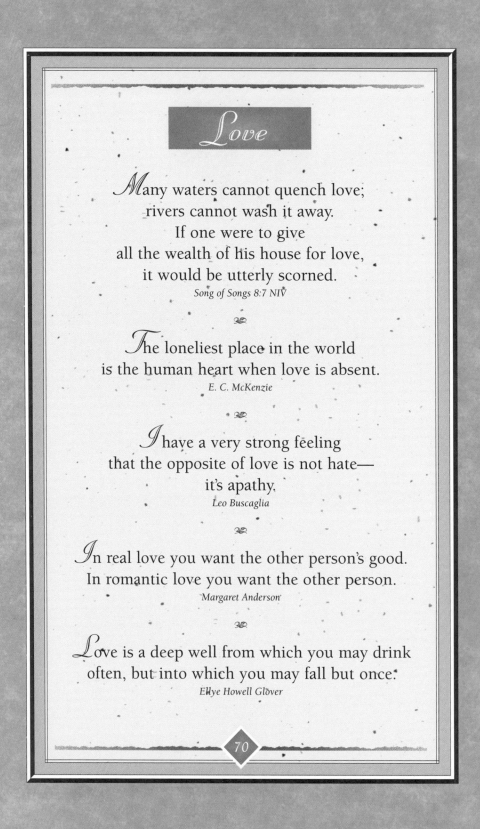

Love

Many waters cannot quench love;
rivers cannot wash it away.
If one were to give
all the wealth of his house for love,
it would be utterly scorned.

Song of Songs 8:7 NIV

The loneliest place in the world
is the human heart when love is absent.

E. C. McKenzie

I have a very strong feeling
that the opposite of love is not hate—
it's apathy.

Leo Buscaglia

In real love you want the other person's good.
In romantic love you want the other person.

Margaret Anderson

Love is a deep well from which you may drink
often, but into which you may fall but once.

Ellye Howell Glover

*L*ove doesn't make the world go round.
Love is what makes the ride worthwhile.
Franklin P. Jones

Love is not a feeling but a choice.
Soren Kierkegaard

*I*t is not our toughness
that keeps us warm at night,
but our tenderness
which makes others want to keep us warm.
Harold Lyon

*L*ove does not consist in gazing at each other,
but in looking outward together
in the same direction.
Antoine de Saint-Exupéry

*I*t is better to have loved and lost,
than not to love at all.
Alfred, Lord Tennyson

Does God love us because we are special—
or are we special because God loves us?
William Arthur Ward

❧

Who, being loved, is poor?
Oscar Wilde

❧

I am not one of those
who do not believe in love at first sight,
but I believe in taking a second look.
Henry Vincent

❧

Love and a cough cannot be hid.
George Herbert

❧

What the world really needs is more love
and less paperwork.
Pearl Bailey

Joy (Happiness)

*T*here is joy
in the presence of the angels of God
over one sinner that repenteth.
Luke 15:10 KJV

❧

*L*aughter is the shortest distance
between two people.
Victor Borge

❧

He who laughs, lasts!
Mary Pettibone Poole

❧

*H*appiness makes up in height
for what it lacks in length.
Robert Frost

*N*o matter how dull, or how mean,
or how wise a man is,
he feels that happiness
is his indisputable right.

Helen Keller

❧

*E*njoy the little things,
for one day you may look back
and realize they were the big things.

Robert Brault

❧

*N*ow and then it's good
to pause in our pursuit of happiness
and just be happy.

Anonymous

❧

Happiness is an inside job.

Anonymous.

❧

*L*aughter is a tranquilizer
with no side effects.

Arnold H. Glasow

*M*ost people are about as happy
as they make up their minds to be.
Abraham Lincoln

❧

*J*oy is the echo of God's life within us.
Joseph Marmion

❧

*I*f you're going to be able to look back on
something and laugh about it,
you might as well laugh about it now.
Marie Osmond

❧

*I*f you have no joy in your religion,
there's a leak in your Christianity somewhere.
Billy Sunday

❧

A laugh is a smile that bursts.
Mary H. Waldrip

*H*appiness is perfume,
you can't pour it on somebody else
without getting a few drops on yourself.
James Van Der Zee

❧

*T*he boy on the sandlot
gets just as big a kick out of a home run
as Babe Ruth.
Will Rogers

❧

Happiness is good health and a bad memory.
Ingrid Bergman

❧

*A*fter being asked if football coach Tom Landry
ever smiles, former player Walt Garrison replied,
"I don't know. I only played there nine years."

Kindness

*Do to others as you
would have them do to you.*
Luke 6:31 NIV

❧

I expect to pass through life but once.
If therefore, there be any kindness I can show,
or any good thing I can do to any fellow being,
let me do it now, and not defer or neglect it,
as I shall not pass this way again.
William Penn

❧

*T*he kindness of some
is too much like an echo:
it returns exactly the counterpart
of what it receives,
and neither more nor less.
Bowes

*Y*ou cannot do a kindness too soon,
for you never know how soon it will be too late.
Ralph Waldo Emerson

❧

*O*ne kind word
can warm three winter months.
Japanese Proverb

❧

*I*t's not true that nice guys finish last.
Nice guys are winners
before the game even starts.
Addison Walker

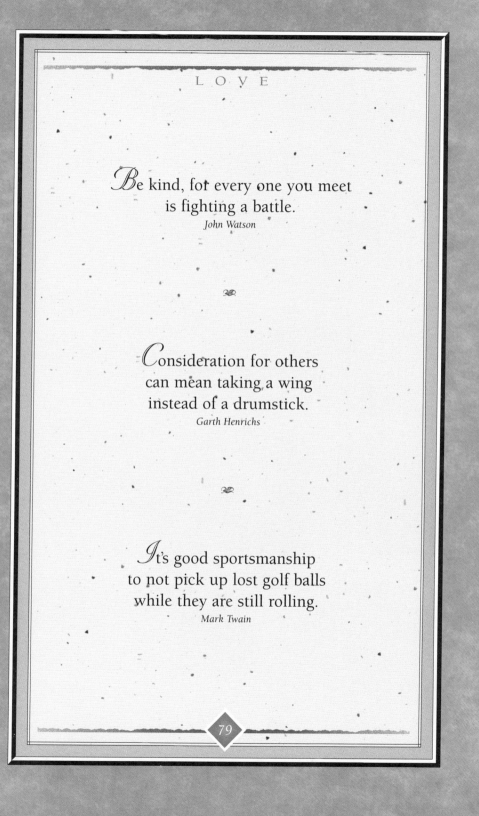

*B*e kind, for every one you meet
is fighting a battle.

John Watson

*C*onsideration for others
can mean taking a wing
instead of a drumstick.

Garth Henrichs

*I*t's good sportsmanship
to not pick up lost golf balls
while they are still rolling.

Mark Twain

Mercy

*L*et me fall into the hands of the LORD,
for his mercy is very great;
but do not let me
fall into the hands of men.

1 Chronicles 21:13 NIV

❧

*F*orgiveness is the fragrance the violet
sheds on the heel that has crushed it.

Mark Twain

❧

To err is human, to forgive, divine.

Alexander Pope

Mourning

They wept until they could weep no more.

1 Samuel 30:4 TLB

❧

The soul would have no rainbow
had the eyes no tears.

John Vance Cheney

❧

On the sands of life sorrow treads heavily,
and leaves a print time cannot wash away.

Henry Neele

❧

Rich tears!
What power lies in those falling drops.

Mary Delarivier Manley

❧

Tears are often the telescope by which men
see far into heaven.

Henry Ward Beecher

*I*n the real dark night of the soul
it is always three o'clock in the morning.
F. Scott Fitzgerald

❧

*T*ake my word for it, the saddest thing
under the sky is a soul incapable of sadness.
Countess de Gasparin

❧

*S*orrow is a fruit:
God does not make it grow on limbs
too weak to bear it.
Hugo

❧

I cannot prevent the birds of sorrow
from passing over my head, but I can keep them
from building a nest in my hair.
Chinese Proverb

❧

*W*hen I'm sad I sing, and then others
can be sad with me.
Mark Twain

NOW
I *know*
I'VE got a
heart,
'CAUSE *it's*
breaking.

❧ ❧ ❧

The Tin Man
(The Wizard of Oz)

Lament

*Oh, my anguish, my anguish! I writhe in pain.
Oh, the agony of my heart! My heart
pounds within me, I cannot keep silent.*
Jeremiah 4:19 NIV

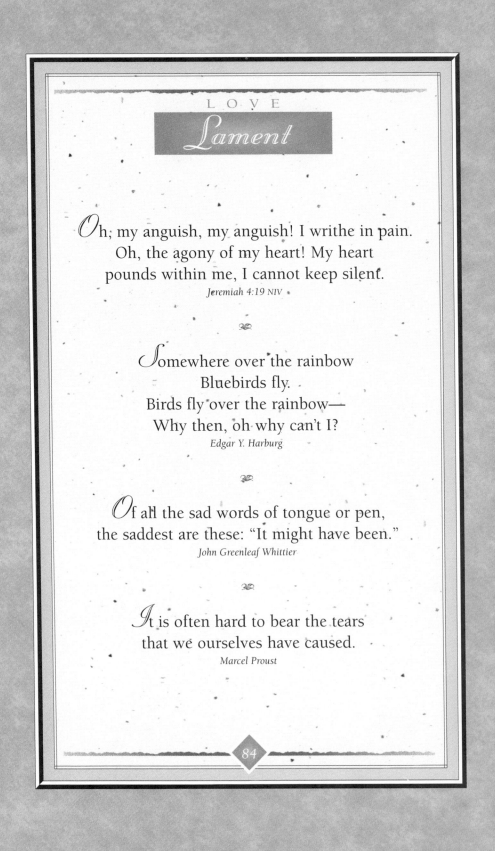

*Somewhere over the rainbow
Bluebirds fly.
Birds fly over the rainbow—
Why then, oh why can't I?*
Edgar Y. Harburg

*Of all the sad words of tongue or pen,
the saddest are these: "It might have been."*
John Greenleaf Whittier

*It is often hard to bear the tears
that we ourselves have caused.*
Marcel Proust

Comfort

*A*s a mother comforts her child,
so will I comfort you....
Isaiah 66:13 NIV

❧

*W*hen things are bad, we take comfort
in the thought that they could always be worse.
And when they are, we find hope in the thought
that things are so bad they have to get better.
Malcolm S. Forbes

❧

*N*oble deeds and hot baths
are the best cures for depression.
Dodie Smith

*I*f you're going to care about the fall
of the sparrow you can't pick and choose
who's going to be the sparrow.
Madeleine L'Engle

❧

*H*ospitality consists in a little fire,
a little food, and an immense quiet.
Ralph Waldo Emerson

❧

*N*othing dries sooner than a tear.
German Proverb

❧

*M*ost of our comforts grow up
between our crosses.
Edward Young

❧

*O*ne reason a dog can be such a comfort
when you're feeling blue
is that he doesn't try to find out why.
Anonymous

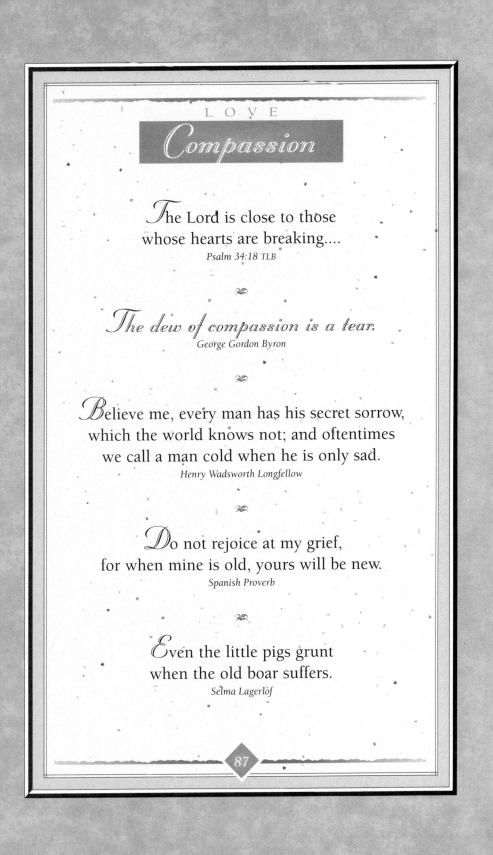

LOVE

Compassion

*T*he Lord is close to those
whose hearts are breaking....
Psalm 34:18 TLB

❧

The dew of compassion is a tear.
George Gordon Byron

❧

*B*elieve me, every man has his secret sorrow,
which the world knows not; and oftentimes
we call a man cold when he is only sad.
Henry Wadsworth Longfellow

❧

*D*o not rejoice at my grief,
for when mine is old, yours will be new.
Spanish Proverb

❧

*E*ven the little pigs grunt
when the old boar suffers.
Selma Lagerlöf

Peace

The wolf will live with the lamb,
the leopard will lie down with the goat,
the calf and the lion and the yearling together;
and a little child will lead them.

Isaiah 11:6 NIV

I am leaving you with a gift—
peace of mind and heart! And the peace I give
isn't fragile like the peace the world gives.

John 14:27 TLB

The mere absence of war is not peace.

John F. Kennedy

They want peace, but they want a gun
to help get it with.

Will Rogers

Where there is peace, God is.

George Herbert

Sympathy

*R*ejoice with them that do rejoice,
and weep with them that weep.
Romans 12:15 KJV

❧

Sympathy is your pain in my heart.
Halford E. Luccock

❧

*W*ho would recognize the unhappy
if grief had no language?
Publilius Syrus

❧

*T*here is no greater loan than a sympathetic ear.
Frank Tyger

❧

*A*nyone can sympathize with the sufferings
of a friend, but it requires a very fine nature
to sympathize with a friend's success.
Oscar Wilde

*A*fter that, he poured water into a basin
and began to wash his disciples' feet,
drying them with the towel
that was wrapped around him.

John 13:5 NIV

*T*he sufficiency of my merit is to know
that my merit is not sufficient.

St. Augustine

*T*he really tough thing about true humility
is you can't brag about it.

Gene Brown

*N*othing is as hard to do gracefully
as getting down off your high horse.

Franklin P. Jones

❧

*T*hose who travel the high road of humility
are not troubled by heavy traffic.

Alan K. Simpson

❧

Sometimes I amaze myself.
I say this humbly.

Don King

Don't
BE humble.
YOU'RE
not THAT
great.

❧ ❧ ❧

Golda Meir

LOVE

Charity

It is more blessed to give than to receive.
Acts 20:35 KJV

❧

Lots of people think they are charitable
if they give away their old clothes
and things they don't want.
Myrtle Reed

❧

The fragrance always remains in the hand
that gives the rose.
Heda Bejar

*T*hat which you cannot give away,
you do not possess. It possesses you.

Ivern Ball

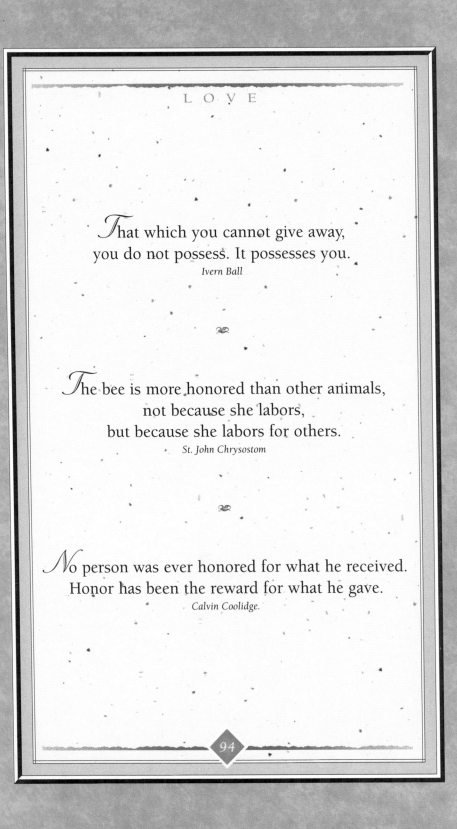

*T*he bee is more honored than other animals,
not because she labors,
but because she labors for others.

St. John Chrysostom

*N*o person was ever honored for what he received.
Honor has been the reward for what he gave.

Calvin Coolidge.

If charity cost no money and benevolence
caused no heartache,
the world would be full of philanthropists.
Yiddish Proverb

⁂

If you haven't any charity in your heart,
you have the worst kind of heart trouble.
Bob Hope

⁂

In Faith and Hope the world will disagree,
But all mankind's concern is Charity.
Alexander Pope

Faith

CHAPTER FOUR

I Can't Do It!

❧ ❧ ❧

How many times have you been around someone whose most famous line would probably be, "I'm going down with the ship!"

Whether it's learning a new piece for a piano contest or a complicated formula in geometry, attitude can be everything. Will I be the one survivor to swim safely to shore or a drowning victim who couldn't keep my head above water?

If God said I can and I believe I can, then all that's left is to do it! I may just be the *one* person who will sail that ship to port! God wants us to have FAITH in Him and ourselves. I may not be able to do it, but...

God and I can do It!
(Because *He* said so!)

Fear

KNOCKED

AT THE door.

Faith

ANSWERED.

NO ONE

WAS there.

❧ ❧ ❧

Anonymous

Faith

I tell you the truth,
if you have faith as small as a mustard seed,
you can say to this mountain,
"Move from here to there" and it will move.
Nothing will be impossible for you.
Matthew 17:20 NIV

❧

Faith is a refusal to panic.
D. Martyn Lloyd-Jones

❧

*T*he object of your faith must be Christ.
Not faith in ritual, not faith in sacrifices,
not faith in morals, not faith in yourself—
not faith in anything but Christ!
Billy Graham

*E*verything that we see is a shadow
cast by that which we do not see.
Martin Luther King, Jr.

❧

*T*rust in God—but tie your camel tight.
Persian Proverb

❧

*S*orrow looks back,
worry looks around,
faith looks up.
Anonymous

Prayer

Very early in the morning, while it was still dark,
Jesus got up, left the house and went off
to a solitary place, where he prayed.

Mark 1:35 NIV

Do not pray for easy lives; pray to be stronger men!
Do not pray for tasks equal to your powers,
pray for powers equal to your tasks....

Phillips Brooks

If you don't have faith, pray anyway.
If you don't understand
or believe the words you're saying,
pray anyway. Prayer can start faith,
particularly if you pray aloud.
And even the most imperfect prayer
is an attempt to reach God.

Cary Grant

Christians and camels
receive their burdens kneeling.

Ambrose Bierce

Any concern too small
to be turned into a prayer
is too small
to be made into a burden.

Corrie ten Boom

❧

In prayer it is better to have
a heart without words,
than words without a heart.

John Bunyan

❧

Prayer does not equip us for greater works—
prayer is the greater work.

Oswald Chambers

❧

And Satan trembles when he sees
The weakest saint upon his knees.

William Cowper

❧

*Just pray for a tough hide
and a tender heart.*

Ruth Bell Graham

*O*h, Adam was a gardener, and God
who made him sees
That half a proper gardener's work is done
upon his knees.
Rudyard Kipling

I have been driven many times to my knees
by the overwhelming conviction
that I had nowhere else to go.
Abraham Lincoln

*L*ord, when we are wrong,
make us willing to change.
And when we are right,
make us easy to live with.
Peter Marshall

*G*roanings which cannot be uttered
are often prayers which cannot be refused.
Charles Spurgeon

More things are wrought by prayer
than this world dreams of.
Alfred, Lord Tennyson

❧

Prayer is not overcoming God's reluctance,
it is laying hold of His highest willingness.
R. C. Trench

❧

The Lord's Prayer is not,
as some fancy, the easiest,
the most natural of all devout utterances.
It may be committed to memory quickly,
but it is slowly learned by heart.
John F. D. Maurice

❧

I have found the perfect antidote for fear.
Whenever it sticks up its ugly face I clobber it
with prayer....
Dale Evans Rogers

Miracles

*A*bout four o'clock in the morning
Jesus came to them, walking on the water!
Matthew 14:25 TLB

❧

*M*ost of us do not understand nuclear fission,
but we accept it. I don't understand television,
but I accept it. I don't understand radio,
but every week my voice goes out around the world,
and I accept it. Why is it so easy to accept
all these man-made miracles and so difficult
to accept the miracles of the Bible?
Billy Graham

❧

*When we do what we can,
God will do what we can't.*
Anonymous

❧

*W*hen somebody tells you nothing is impossible,
ask him to dribble a football.
Anonymous

Courage

*H*ave I not commanded you?
Be strong and courageous. Do not be terrified;
do not be discouraged, for the LORD your God
will be with you wherever you go.

Joshua 1:9 NIV

*C*ourage is not the towering oak
that sees storms come and go;
it is the fragile blossom
that opens in the snow.

Alice Machenzie Swaim

Courage is grace under pressure.

Ernest Hemingway

I'd rather give my life than be afraid to give it.

Lyndon B. Johnson

The only thing we have to fear is fear itself.
Franklin D. Roosevelt

❧

He who loses wealth loses much;
he who loses a friend loses more;
but he that loses his courage loses all.
Miguel de Cervantes

❧

Don't be afraid to take big steps.
You can't cross a chasm in two small jumps.
David Lloyd George

❧

I've learned to admit it when I'm scared
because it takes courage to know
when you ought to be afraid.
James A. Michener

*P*ain nourishes courage.
You can't be brave if you've only had
wonderful things happen to you.
Mary Tyler Moore

*O*ften the test of courage is not to die but to live.
Vittorio Alfieri

*C*owards die many times before their death;
the valiant never taste of death but once.
William Shakespeare

*C*ourage is resistance to fear, mastery of fear,
not absence of fear.
Mark Twain

There's no substitute for guts.
Paul "Bear" Bryant

Confession

*N*ow make confession to the LORD,
the God of your fathers, and do his will.

Ezra 10:11 NIV

❧

*L*et my heart be broken by the things
that break the heart of God.

Bob Pierce

❧

I make mistakes; I'll be the second to admit it.

Jean Kerr

❧

*W*e're all proud of making little mistakes.
It gives us the feeling
we don't make any big ones.

Andrew A. Rooney

Repentance

*R*epent! Turn away from all your offenses;
then sin will not be your downfall. Rid yourselves
of all the offenses you have committed,
and get a new heart and a new spirit.

Ezekiel 18:30-31 NIV

*T*here is one case of death-bed
repentance recorded—the penitent thief—
that no one should despair; and only one,
that no one should presume.

St. Augustine

To do it no more is the truest repentance.

Martin Luther

*M*any persons who appear to repent
are like sailors who throw their goods overboard
in a storm, and wish for them again in a calm.

Mead

I once shook hands with Pat Boone
and my whole right side sobered up.

Dean Martin

FAITH

Fasting

And now about fasting. When you fast,
declining your food for a spiritual purpose,
don't do it publicly, as the hypocrites do....
Matthew 6:16 TLB

❧

*The best of all medicines
are resting and fasting.*
Benjamin Franklin

Healing

The report of his miracles
spread far beyond the borders of Galilee
so that sick folk
were soon coming to be healed
from as far away as Syria.
And whatever their illness and pain,
or if they were possessed by demons,
or were insane, or paralyzed—
he healed them all.

Matthew 4:24 TLB

❧

I treated him, God cured him.

Ambroise Paré

❧

God heals, and the doctor takes the fee.

Benjamin Franklin

Hope

*L*et us hold unswervingly
to the hope we profess,
for he who promised is faithful.

Hebrews 10:23 NIV

❧

*T*o eat bread without hope
is still slowly to starve to death.

Pearl S. Buck

❧

If it were not for hopes, the heart would break.

Thomas Fuller

❧

*W*hen you say a situation or a person is hopeless,
you are slamming the door in the face of God.

Charles L. Allen

❧

*T*he message of dawn is hope.

Winston Churchill

❧

*Y*ou cannot put a great hope into a small soul.

J. L. Jones

FAITH

*W*e must accept finite disappointment,
but we must never lose infinite hope.

Martin Luther King, Jr.

❧

*H*ope is the best part of our riches. —
What sufficeth it that we have the wealth
of the Indies in our pockets,
if we have not the hope of heaven in our souls?

Bovee

❧

*S*ome people grumble because roses have thorns.
I am thankful that thorns have roses.

Karr

❧

*S*wing hard, in case they throw the ball
where you're swinging.

Duke Snider

❧

*W*hen down in the mouth remember Jonah—
he came out all right!

Thomas Edison

❧

It ain't over till it's over.

Lawrence "Yogi" Berra

Confidence

I can do all things through Christ
which strengtheneth me.
Philippians 4:13 KJV

A man who wants to lead the orchestra
must turn his back on the crowd.
Anonymous

*M*y mother said to me, "If you become a soldier
you'll be a general; if you become a monk
you'll end up as the pope." Instead,
I became a painter and wound up as Picasso.
Pablo Picasso

*S*hoot for the moon. Even if you miss it
you will land among the stars.
Les Brown

NO bird
soars TOO
high
IF HE soars
WITH his own
wings.

❧ ❧ ❧

William Blake

*We are all worms, but I do believe
I am a glowworm.*
Winston Churchill

❧

When I was in the batter's box,
I felt sorry for the pitcher.
Roger Hornsby

❧

I've never lost a game in my life.
Once in a while, time ran out on me.
Bobby Layne

If you don't have confidence,
you'll always find a way not to win.
Carl Lewis

❧

If I only had a little humility I would be perfect.
Ted Turner

❧

*H*eads I win, tails you lose.
Anonymous

Conviction

*A*nd when the centurion,
who stood there in front of Jesus,
heard his cry and saw how he died, he said,
"Surely this man was the Son of God!"
Mark 15:39 NIV

*I*n matters of style, swim with the current;
in matters of principle, stand like a rock.
Thomas Jefferson

*R*ight is right, even if everyone is against it,
and wrong is wrong, even if everyone is for it.
William Penn

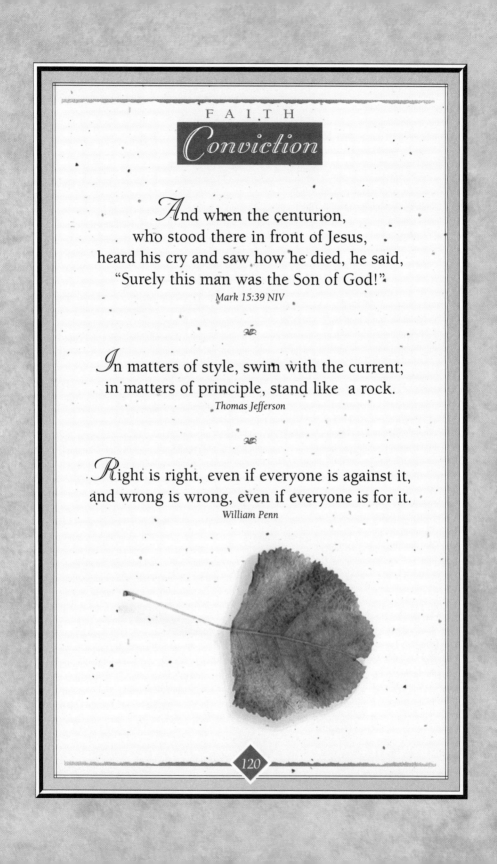

FAITH

*I*t's easy to make a buck.
It's a lot tougher to make a difference.
Tom Brokaw

❧

Give me liberty or give me death!
Patrick Henry

❧

*W*hy is it the ship beats the waves
when the waves are so many
and the ship is one?
The reason is that ship has a purpose.
Winston Churchill

❧

*T*he ripest peach is highest on the tree.
James Whitcomb Riley

Ah, but a man's reach should exceed his grasp,
Or what's a heaven for?
Robert Browning

❧

We're going to get in
two hours of good practice
even if it takes six hours.
Lou Holtz

❧

Winning isn't everything,
but it beats anything that comes in second.
Paul "Bear" Bryant

❧

I wouldn't ever set out
to hurt anybody deliberately unless it was,
you know, important—
like a league game or something.
Dick Butkus

Belief

Jesus told them, "This is the will of God,
that you believe in the one he has sent."
John 6:29 TLB

❦

Some things have to be believed to be seen.
Ralph Hodgson

❦

I believe the promises of God
enough to venture an eternity on them.
G. Campbell Morgan

❦

One person with a belief is equal to a force of 99
who only have interest.
John Stuart Mill

❦

To be a great champion
you must believe you are the best.
If you're not, pretend you are.
Muhammad Ali

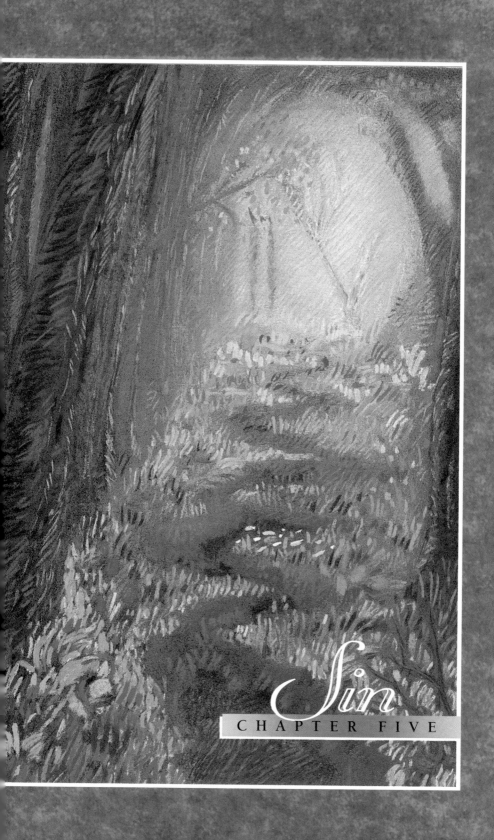

Sin

CHAPTER FIVE

Do You Hate The Right Things?

❧ ❧ ❧

*P*ickled beets never was my favorite dish. Okay, I guess it's fair to say I hated them. I don't know why I couldn't have hated coconut cream pie or chocolate glazed donuts—my personal breakfast of champions.

Some people dislike boxing as a sport, some bell-bottom slacks, others rainy days or Mondays. I suppose we all have things which are less than our favorites. But what do you really hate?

Did you know there are some things God hates? According to the Bible, God *hates* pride, lying, and hypocrisy, just to name a few. And with a passion! But He never stops loving us. So while vehemently against those things, those attitudes, and those actions which can hurt us, His love for the person is always there. In other words, God hates the sin but He still loves the sinner.

Can we learn to hate sin like that? Sure we can. As the Apostle Paul matured through the years, his progressive comments concerning himself went from "the least of the apostles" to "less than the least of all saints" to "chief of all sinners." He grew so close to the Lord that all SIN in his life was magnified by the brilliance of God's perfect Son. We must remember that if we love the S-O-N rightly, then we will...

Hate the S-I-N.

To *walk*

OUT OF

God's *will*

IS TO

step INTO

nowhere.

❧ ❧ ❧

C. S. Lewis

Sin

For all have sinned,
and come short of the glory of God.

Romans 3:23 KJV

❧

Sins are like circles in the water when a stone
is thrown into it; one produces another. When anger
was in Cain's heart, murder was not far off.

Philip Henry

❧

Sin is not hurtful because it is forbidden,
but it is forbidden because it is hurtful.

Benjamin Franklin

❧

Don't cover your sins; don't hide them.
You cannot dig a grave so deep but that they
will have a resurrection some time.

D. L. Moody

❧

How immense appear to us the sins
that we have not committed.

Madame Necker

❧

Sin is blatant mutiny against God.
Oswald Chambers

Evil

*E*ven on his bed he plots evil;
he commits himself to a sinful course
and does not reject what is wrong.

Psalm 36:4 NIV

*T*he only thing necessary for the triumph of evil is
for good men to do nothing.

Edmund Burke

*N*o man ever became extremely wicked all at once.

Juvenal

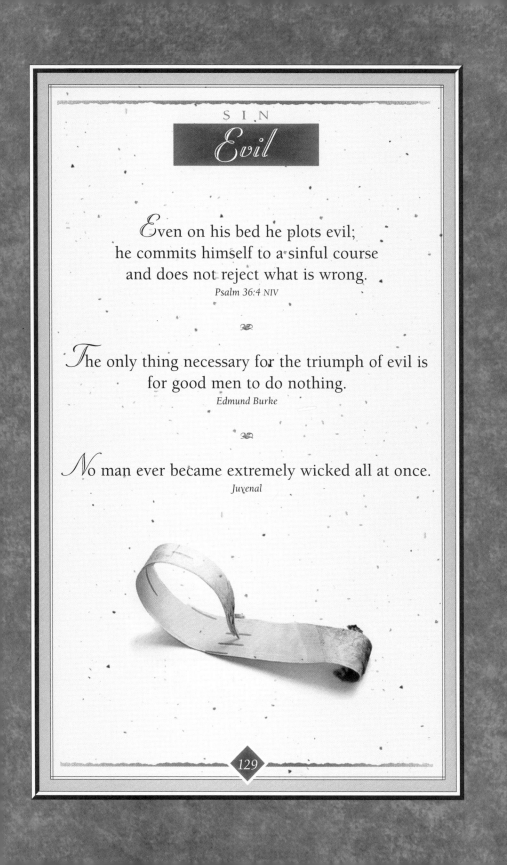

When you choose the lesser of two evils,
always remember that it is still an evil.
Max Lerner

Pity the criminal all you like,
but don't call evil good.
Feodor Dostoevski

Evil often triumphs but it never conquers.
J. Roux

As surely as God is good,
so surely there is no such thing as necessary evil.
Robert Southey

Hear no evil, see no evil, speak no evil.
Legend related to the "Three Wise Monkeys"

The wickedness of the world is so great
you have to run your legs off
to avoid having them stolen from under you.
Bertolt Brecht

Judgment of the Ungodly

The end is now upon you
and I will unleash my anger against you.
I will judge you according to your conduct
and repay you for all your detestable practices.
Ezekiel 7:3 NIV

❧

Punishment is justice for the unjust.
St. Augustine

❧

God's mill grinds slow but sure.
George Herbert

❧

Make no judgments where you
have no compassion.
Anne McCaffrey

❧

Out of the frying-pan into the fire.
Tertullian

The sin ye do by two and two
ye must pay for one by one.
Rudyard Kipling

Vice carries a sting in its tail, like the scorpion.
D. L. Moody

He that lieth down with dogs,
shall rise up with fleas.
Benjamin Franklin

While forbidden fruit is said to taste sweeter,
it usually spoils faster.
Abigail Van Buren

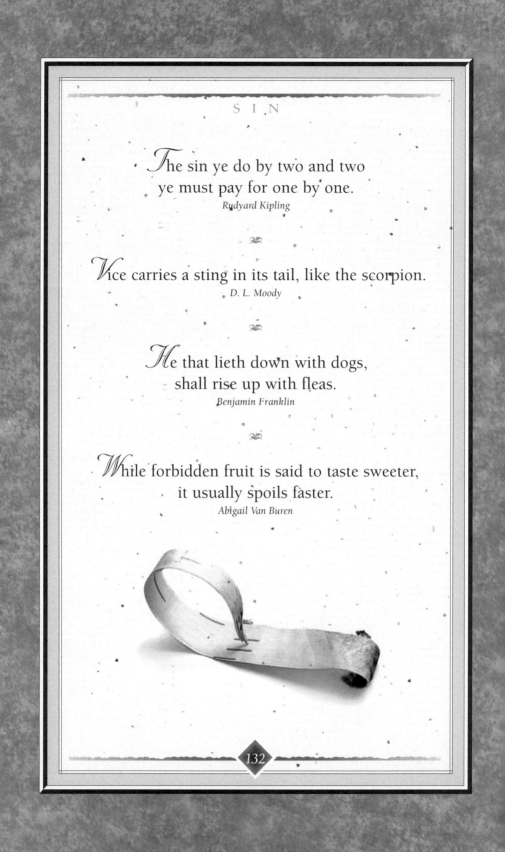

Death

*T*here is a way that seems right to a man,
but in the end it leads to death.

Proverbs 14:12 NIV

❧

*T*hough it be in the power of the weakest arm
to take away life, it is not in the strongest
to deprive us of death.

Sir Thomas Browne

❧

*W*e go to the grave of a friend, saying,
"A man is dead;" but angels throng about him,
saying, "A man is born."

Henry Ward Beecher

❧

*T*he Christian, at his death, should not be like the
child who is forced by the rod to quit his play,
but like one who is wearied of it
and is willing to go home.

Gotthold

❧

*O*ther appointments in life we can neglect or break,
but here is an appointment that no man can ignore,
no man can break.

Billy Graham

Death did not first strike Adam,
the first sinful man; nor Cain, the first murderer:
but Abel, the innocent and righteous.
Bishop Hall

❧

Death is not a period
but a comma in the story of life.
Amos J. Tarver

❧

Death is the golden key
that opens the palace of eternity.
John Milton

❧

Death is a camel that lies down at every door.
Persian Proverb

❧

Each departed friend is a magnet
that attracts us to the next world.
Jean Paul Richter

*I*s death the last sleep?
No, it is the last and final awakening.
Sir Walter Scott

🙿

*L*et us endeavour so to live
that when we come to die
even the undertaker will be sorry.
Mark Twain

🙿

I'm not afraid to die.
I just don't want to be there when it happens.
Woody Allen

🙿

*E*ither this man is dead or my watch has stopped.
Groucho Marx

🙿

Get my Swan costume ready.
Anna Pavlova (Last Words)

Hell

For God did not spare
even the angels who sinned,
but threw them into hell,
chained in gloomy caves and darkness
until the judgment day.

2 Peter 2:4 TLB

People seem to sleep and to forget
that there is no door out of hell.
If they enter there they must remain,
age after age. Millions on millions of years
will roll on, but there will be no door,
no escape out of hell.

D. L. Moody

All *hope* ABANDON, *ye* WHO *enter* HERE!

❧ ❧ ❧

Dante

The safest road to hell is the gradual one—
the gentle slope, soft underfoot,
without sudden turnings,
without milestones,
without signposts.

C. S. Lewis

❧

Hell, essentially and basically,
is banishment from the presence of God
for deliberately rejecting Jesus Christ
as Lord and Savior.

Billy Graham

❧

The hottest spots in hell
are reserved for those who never take sides.

Dante

❧

People in hell,
where do they tell people to go?

Red Skelton

Curses

Cursed is the one who trusts in man,
who depends on flesh for his
strength
and whose heart turns away from
the LORD.

Jeremiah 17:5 NIV

❧

It is never wise to seek or wish
for another's misfortune.
If malice or envy were tangible and had a shape,
it would be the shape of a boomerang.

Charley Reese

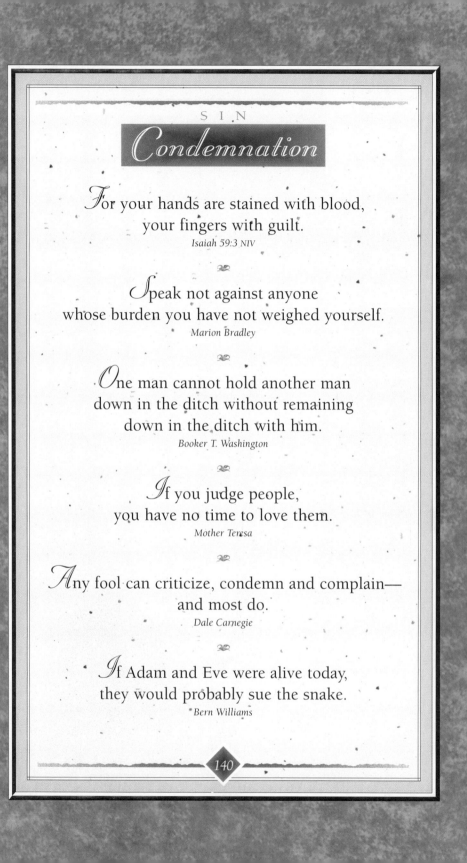

SIN

Condemnation

For your hands are stained with blood,
your fingers with guilt.
Isaiah 59:3 NIV

❧

Speak not against anyone
whose burden you have not weighed yourself.
Marion Bradley

❧

One man cannot hold another man
down in the ditch without remaining
down in the ditch with him.
Booker T. Washington

❧

If you judge people,
you have no time to love them.
Mother Teresa

❧

Any fool can criticize, condemn and complain—
and most do.
Dale Carnegie

❧

If Adam and Eve were alive today,
they would probably sue the snake.
Bern Williams

Temptation

*B*ut every man is tempted,
when he is drawn away of his own lust,
and enticed.

James 1:14 KJV

❧

*T*o pray against temptations, and yet to rush into
occasions, is to thrust your fingers into the fire,
and then pray they might not be burnt.

Thomas Secker

❧

*P*refer a loss to a dishonest gain;
the one brings pain at the moment,
the other for all time.

Chilton

❧

*No degree of temptation
justifies any degree of sin.*

N. P. Willis

Better shun the bait than struggle in the snare.

John Dryden

※

Few speed records are broken
when people run from temptation.

E. C. McKenzie

※

Most people want to be delivered from temptation,
but would like to keep in touch.

Robert Orben

※

The trouble with opportunity is that it only knocks.
Temptation kicks the door in.

Anonymous

※

To cease smoking is the easiest thing I ever did.
I ought to know because I've done it
a thousand times.

Mark Twain

Unbelief

I have spoken to you of earthly things
and you do not believe; how then will you
believe if I speak of heavenly things?

John 3:12 NIV

※

*T*here are no atheists in the foxholes.

William Thomas Cummings

※

*N*ever put a question mark
where God has put a period.

John R. Rice

※

*A*n atheist is a man who has no invisible means
of support.

Fulton J. Sheen

※

*A*theism is rather in the lip
than in the heart of man.

Francis Bacon

※

All unbelief is the belief of a lie.

Horatius Bonar

Hatred

*I*f the world hate you,
ye know that it
hated me before it hated you.
John 15:18 KJV

*A*lways remember others may hate you
but those who hate you don't win unless you
hate them. And then you destroy yourself.
Richard M. Nixon

*H*ating people is like burning down
your own house to get rid of a rat.
Harry Emerson Fosdick

*H*atred is the rabid dog
that turns on its owner.
Revenge is the raging fire
that consumes the arsonist.
Bitterness is the trap
that snares the hunter.

Max Lucado

❧

*H*ate is ravening vulture beaks descending
on a place of skulls.

Amy Lowell

❧

I never hated a man enough to give him
his diamonds back.

Zsa Zsa Gabor

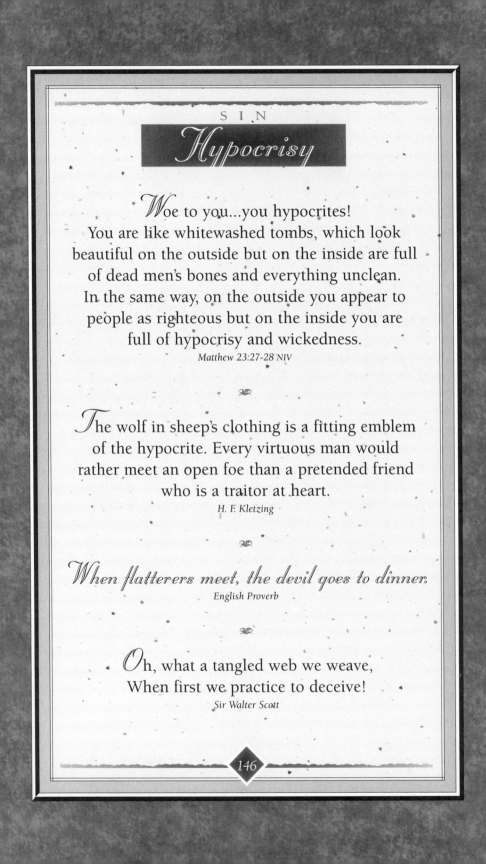

Hypocrisy

*W*oe to you...you hypocrites!
You are like whitewashed tombs, which look
beautiful on the outside but on the inside are full
of dead men's bones and everything unclean.
In the same way, on the outside you appear to
people as righteous but on the inside you are
full of hypocrisy and wickedness.

Matthew 23:27-28 NIV

❧

*T*he wolf in sheep's clothing is a fitting emblem
of the hypocrite. Every virtuous man would
rather meet an open foe than a pretended friend
who is a traitor at heart.

H. F. Kletzing

❧

When flatterers meet, the devil goes to dinner.

English Proverb

❧

*O*h, what a tangled web we weave,
When first we practice to deceive!

Sir Walter Scott

To call myself a Christian
and then not strive to be the best I can be
and do the most I can with what has been given me
would be the height of hypocrisy.
Being a Christian is no excuse for mediocrity....
Orel Hershiser

I cannot give you the formula for success,
but I can give you the formula for failure—
which is: Try to please everybody.
Herbert Bayard Swope

Most people have seen worse things in private
than they pretend to be shocked at in public.
Edgar Watson Howe

Hypocrite: Someone who complains that there
is too much sex and violence on his VCR.
Anonymous

ONE

may *smile,*

AND smile,

and *be a*

villain.

❧ ❧ ❧

William Shakespeare

Apostasy

*I*f we deliberately keep on sinning
after we have received the knowledge of the truth,
no sacrifice for sins is left....

Hebrews 10:26 NIV

*T*he Christian life is never static.
One must either grow in grace,
or there will be backsliding and deterioration.

Henry A. Ironside

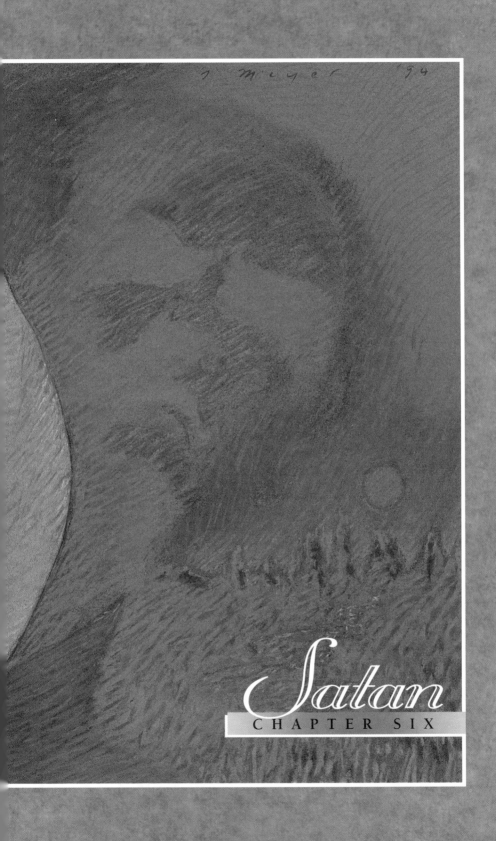

Satan
CHAPTER SIX

Satan's Job Made Easy

❧ ❧ ❧

"I love it! It's the sharpest car on the lot!" the teenager said excitedly to her parents as they bought her graduation present. "I can't wait to show it off to my friends."

"This cruise will be one you'll never forget. And the shopping's fantastic. Those islands have buys you won't believe! But just stay clear of the begging kids. They won't leave you alone."

"He eats, sleeps, and dreams baseball," said the proud dad. "That's all he ever thinks about. Why, his little league team is in contention for the state title!"

Meanwhile...

Satan slinks back and sneers, "Ah, this is one more Christian family I won't have to worry about living abundantly. Why, they're totally wrapped up in themselves. The idol of materialism has captured their hearts, and selfishness is ruling their minds. God is far from their thoughts, and that's how I want it!

"My job is done, for now."

Satan
HIMSELF
masquerades
AS AN
ANGEL
OF light.

❧ ❧ ❧

2 Corinthians 11:14 NIV

Satan

Satan was the first that practised falsehood
under saintly show.
John Milton

❦

Satan is no fool; his timing is good; he waits until
you are in deep trouble, and then he lets you have it.
Dale Evans Rogers

False Teachers

Woe unto them that call evil good, and good evil;
that put darkness for light, and light for darkness;
that put bitter for sweet, and sweet for bitter!
Isaiah 5:20 KJV

❦

Their teaching will spread like gangrene....
2 Timothy 2:17 NIV

❦

Cursed be all that learning
that is contrary to the cross of Christ.
James Madison

Idolatry

*T*heir gods are merely manmade things
of silver and of gold. They can't talk or see,
despite their eyes and mouths! Nor can they hear,
nor smell, nor use their hands or feet, nor speak! And
those who make and worship them
are just as foolish as their idols are.

Psalm 115:4-8 TLB

*O*thers try to worship things that are less than God;
it may be money, or ambition, or drugs, or sex.
In the end they find that they are worthless idols.

Desmond Tutu

*A*nything that comes between me and God
is an idol—anything....

D. L. Moody

Destruction of Idols

*Y*ou must not worship the gods of these other
nations, nor sacrifice to them in any way, and you
must not follow the evil example of these heathen
people; you must utterly conquer them and break
down their shameful idols.

Exodus 23:24 TLB

Demons

Jesus cut him short. "Be silent!" he told the demon.
"Come out!" The demon threw the man to the floor
as the crowd watched, and then left him
without hurting him further.

Luke 4:35 TLB

Devil

Be sober, be vigilant; because your adversary
the devil, as a roaring lion, walketh about,
seeking whom he may devour....

1 Peter 5:8 KJV

❧

The devil never seems so busy
as where the saints are.

Elizabeth Rundle Charles

❧

The devil hath power to assume a pleasing shape.

William Shakespeare

❧

It is not pleasant to believe that there is a personal
devil, but the question is not what is pleasant to
believe but what is true.

R. A. Torrey

Serpent

So the LORD God said to the serpent,
"Because you have done this,
Cursed are you above all the livestock
and all the wild animals!
You will crawl on your belly
and you will eat dust
all the days of your life."

Genesis 3:14 NIV

❧

Sin is like the little serpent aspis,
which stings men, whereby they fall
into a pleasant sleep, and in that sleep die.

Swinnock

❧

The snake stood up for evil in the Garden.

Robert Frost

Evil Spirits

*For we are not fighting against people
made of flesh and blood,
but against persons without bodies—
the evil rulers of the unseen world,
those mighty satanic beings and great evil princes
of darkness who rule this world;
and against huge numbers of wicked spirits
in the spirit world.*

Ephesians 6:12 TLB

*It is a dangerous thing to arouse the evil spirit.
It will turn against and rend you.*

Kelly Miller

False Prophets

Then the LORD said to me, "The prophets
are prophesying lies in my name. I have not sent
them or appointed them or spoken to them. They
are prophesying to you false visions, divinations,
idolatries and the delusions of their own minds."

Jeremiah 14:14 NIV

Beware of false prophets,
which come to you in sheep's clothing,
but inwardly they are ravening wolves.

Matthew 7:15 KJV

Self-imposed deification is as deceiving as a rooster
which thinks that day breaks because he crows.

D. E. King

False Worship

Be careful, or you will be enticed to turn away
and worship other gods and bow down to them.

Deuteronomy 11:16 NIV

First and foremost, the belief systems of the cults
are characterized by closed-mindedness.

Walter Martin

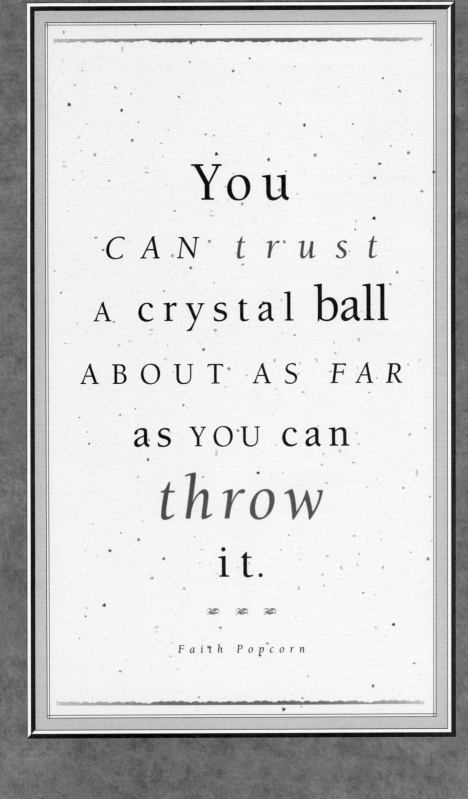

You
CAN trust
A crystal ball
ABOUT AS FAR
as YOU can
throw
it.

Faith Popcorn

Witchcraft

*L*et no one be found among you
who sacrifices his son or daughter in the fire,
who practices divination or sorcery,
interprets omens, engages in witchcraft,
or casts spells, or who is a medium or spiritist
or who consults the dead. Anyone
who does these things is detestable to the LORD....

Deuteronomy 18:10-12 NIV

*T*o deny the possibility, nay, the actual existence
of witchcraft and sorcery is flatly to contradict
the revealed word of God.

William Blackstone

Antichrist

*H*e will oppose and will exalt himself
over everything that is called God or is worshiped,
so that he sets himself up in God's temple,
proclaiming himself to be God.

2 Thessalonians 2:4 NIV

Salvation

CHAPTER SEVEN

I Need a Life Preserver

※ ※ ※

Who could have guessed that such a huge ship—the showpiece of the seas—would meet disaster when a 200-foot tidal wave crashed and beat against it?

This had to be a dream, a nightmare! But the cries for help were too real. People—men and women, boys and girls. People who just moments before were laughing, planning, and sleeping were now being tossed into that bottomless pit, that ocean black with the night.

I wanted to help. I really did. Their pleading for SALVATION, their screams for someone to throw them a life preserver, could not be ignored. But it was too late!

Spiritually, too, people are crying out for someone to throw them a life preserver. They are sinking into a silent pit of despair, loneliness, and fear. They don't have the answers. But, hope is ever before them. Jesus Christ is the way, the truth, and the life. He is the life preserver so many are grasping for.

Jesus is salvation for your sinking ship.

THE
saints
ARE THE
sinners WHO
KEEP ON
going.

❧ ❧ ❧

Robert Louis Stevenson

Salvation

*T*here is salvation in no one else!
Under all heaven there is no other name for men
to call upon to save them.
Acts 4:12 TLB

❧

*T*he cross is the only ladder
high enough to touch Heaven's threshold.
G. D. Boardman

❧

*P*erhaps the straight and narrow path would be
wider if more people used it.
Kay Ingram

❧

*T*he elect are whosoever will, and the nonelect,
whosoever won't.
Henry Ward Beecher

❧

A man may go to heaven without health, without
riches, without honors, without learning, without
friends, but he can never go there without Christ.
John Dyer

❧

*H*e who provides for this life, but takes no care for
eternity, is wise for a moment, but a fool forever.
John Tillotson

*B*lessings in the city,
Blessings in the field;...
Blessings when you come in,
Blessings when you go out.

Deuteronomy 28:3-6 TLB

*R*eflect upon your present blessings,
of which every man has many:
not on your past misfortunes,
of which all men have some.

Charles Dickens

*Let me tell you that every misery I miss
is a new blessing.*
Izaak Walton

❧

May you have warmth in your igloo,
oil in your lamp, and peace in your heart.
Eskimo Proverb

❧

Some people are always telegraphing to heaven
for God to send a cargo of blessing to them,
but they are not at the wharfside
to unload the vessel when it comes.
F. B. Meyer

❧

Blessed is the person who is too busy to worry
in the daytime and too sleepy to worry at night.
Leo Aikman

❧

Blessed are the flexible,
for they shall not be bent out of shape.
Michael McGriff

Deliverance

*Y*ou are my hiding place;
you will protect me from trouble
and surround me with songs of deliverance.

Psalm 32:7 NIV

*W*hen we let freedom ring, when we let it ring
from every village and every hamlet, from every
state and every city, we will be able to speed up
that day when all of God's children, black men
and white men, Jews and Gentiles, Protestants
and Catholics, will be able to join hands and sing
in the words of the old Negro spiritual,
"Free at last! Free at last! Thank God Almighty,
we are free at last!"

Martin Luther King, Jr.

*M*orality may keep you out of jail,
but it takes the blood of Jesus Christ
to keep you out of hell.

Charles Spurgeon

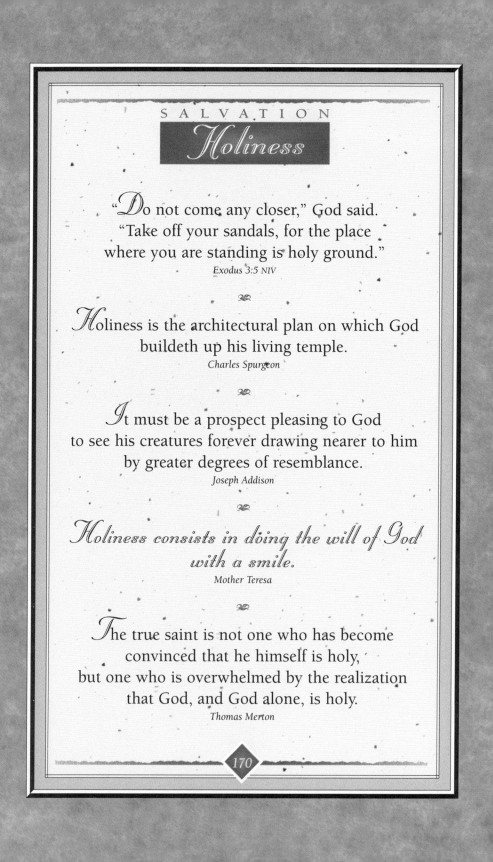

Holiness

"Do not come any closer," God said.
"Take off your sandals, for the place
where you are standing is holy ground."

Exodus 3:5 NIV

Holiness is the architectural plan on which God
buildeth up his living temple.

Charles Spurgeon

It must be a prospect pleasing to God
to see his creatures forever drawing nearer to him
by greater degrees of resemblance.

Joseph Addison

Holiness consists in doing the will of God
with a smile.

Mother Teresa

The true saint is not one who has become
convinced that he himself is holy,
but one who is overwhelmed by the realization
that God, and God alone, is holy.

Thomas Merton

Heaven

*A*nd God shall wipe away all tears from their eyes;
and there shall be no more death, neither sorrow,
nor crying, neither shall there be any more pain:
for the former things are passed away.

Revelation 21:4 KJV

❧

*T*here are no crownwearers in Heaven
that were not crossbearers here below.

Charles Spurgeon

❧

*H*eaven is a prepared place
for a prepared people.

D. L. Moody

❧

Earth has no sorrow that heaven cannot heal.

Thomas Moore

*N*othing is farther than the earth from heaven;
nothing is nearer than heaven to earth.

August W. Hare

*I*f God hath made this world so fair,
where sin and death abound,
how beautiful, beyond compare,
will paradise be found.

Robert Montgomery

the Tabernacle

I have chosen and consecrated this temple
so that my Name may be there forever.
My eyes and my heart will always be there.

2 Chronicles 7:16 NIV

Angels

See, I am sending an angel ahead of you
to guard you along the way and to bring you
to the place I have prepared.

Exodus 23:20 NIV

❦

*Be not forgetful to entertain strangers: for
thereby some have entertained angels unawares.*

Hebrews 13:2 KJV

❦

But men must know that in this theater of man's
life it is reserved only for God and angels
to be lookers on.

Francis Bacon

❦

The angel fetched Peter out of prison,
but it was prayer that fetched the angel.

Thomas Watson

For
fools RUSH

in where

angels

fear TO

tread.

❧ ❧ ❧

Alexander Pope

Eternity

So we fix our eyes not on what is seen,
but on what is unseen.
For what is seen is temporary,
but what is unseen is eternal.
2 Corinthians 4:18 NIV

❧

Eternity is in love with the production of time.
William Blake

❧

The truest end of life
is to know the life that never ends.
William Penn

❧

Where will you be sitting in eternity?
Smoking or Non?
Anonymous

Resurrection

*Y*et we have this assurance:
Those who belong to God shall live again.
Their bodies shall rise again! Those who dwell
in the dust shall awake and sing for joy!
For God's light of life will fall like dew upon them!

Isaiah 26:19 TLB

*U*p from the grave He arose,
With a mighty triumph o'er His foes;
He arose a victor from the dark domain,
And He lives forever with His saints to reign.

Robert Lowry

*O*ur Lord has written the promise
of the resurrection not in books alone,
but in every leaf in the springtime.

Martin Luther

Second Coming

*F*or as the lightning flashes across the sky
from east to west, so shall my coming be,
when I, the Messiah, return.

Matthew 24:27 TLB

*T*he sky shall unfold,
preparing His entrance;
The stars shall applaud Him
with thunders of praise.
The sweet light in His eyes
shall enhance those awaiting;
And we shall behold Him,
then face to face.

Dottie Rambo

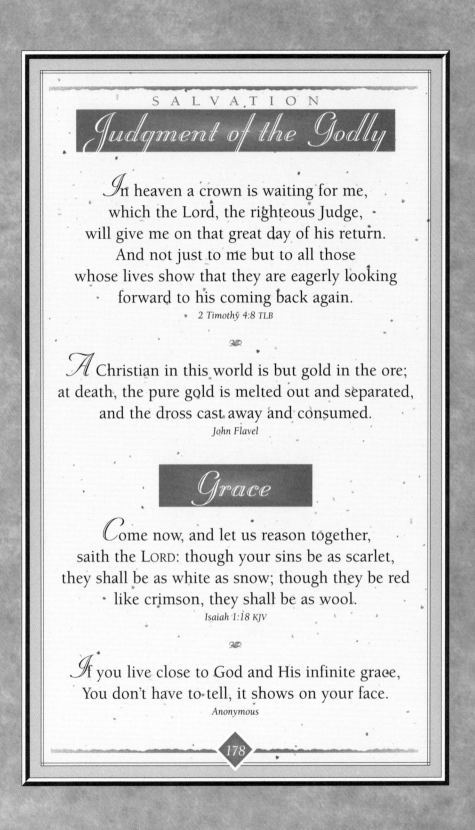

Judgment of the Godly

In heaven a crown is waiting for me,
which the Lord, the righteous Judge,
will give me on that great day of his return.
And not just to me but to all those
whose lives show that they are eagerly looking
forward to his coming back again.

2 Timothy 4:8 TLB

A Christian in this world is but gold in the ore;
at death, the pure gold is melted out and separated,
and the dross cast away and consumed.

John Flavel

Grace

Come now, and let us reason together,
saith the LORD: though your sins be as scarlet,
they shall be as white as snow; though they be red
like crimson, they shall be as wool.

Isaiah 1:18 KJV

If you live close to God and His infinite grace,
You don't have to tell, it shows on your face.

Anonymous

*G*race is but glory begun,
and glory is but grace perfected.
Jonathan Edwards

❧

*C*arry the cross patiently,
and with perfect submission;
and in the end it shall carry you.
Thomas à Kempis

❧

*A*mazing grace! how sweet the sound,
That saved a wretch like me!
I once was lost, but now am found,
Was blind, but now I see.
John Newton

❧

*T*he refiner is never very far from the mouth
of the furnace when his gold is in the fire.
Charles Spurgeon

❧

*T*here is, by God's grace,
an immeasurable distance
between late and too late.
Madam Swetchine

Family

CHAPTER EIGHT

I HAVE THE PERFECT FAMILY!

❧ ❧ ❧

Wouldn't we all love to hear those words spoken often and meant from the heart. Unfortunately, family life is often far from perfect. The "perfect" image lasts about as long as it takes to make it in the front door and confront a house that has either been demolished by three kids and their respective friends or has been ransacked by a prowler. Most of us would probably attribute it to the former. And that's when the image shatters. Mom, Dad, and the kids are battling it out!

Yes, a perfect family life may be all but impossible to achieve, but we can agree there's always room for improvement! God has a lot to say about parents, children, and our relationships with others.

Find some encouragement in this "FAMILY" chapter.

Just follow the Yellow "Quote" Road!

There
is NOTHING
more **sad**
OR *glorious*
than GENERATIONS
changing hands.

❧ ❧ ❧

John Cougar Mellencamp

Family

Marry and have children, and then find mates
for them and have many grandchildren.
Multiply! Don't dwindle away!
Jeremiah 29:6 TLB

❧

Where does the family start?
It starts with a young man falling in love with a girl.
No superior alternative has yet been found.
Winston Churchill

❧

Nobody can do for little children
what grandparents do. Grandparents sort of
sprinkle stardust over the lives of little children.
Alex Haley

❧

Happy families are all alike; every unhappy family
is unhappy in its own way.
Leo N. Tolstoy

❧

Men have sight; women insight.
Victor Hugo

God has no grandchildren.
Anonymous

❧

A grandmother is a person
with too much wisdom to let that stop her
from making a fool of herself
over her grandchildren.
Phil Moss

❧

*G*randchildren don't make a man feel old;
it's the knowledge that he's married to a grandmother.
G. Norman Collie

❧

*T*o be seventy years young
is sometimes far more cheerful and hopeful
than to be forty years old.
Oliver Wendell Holmes, Sr.

❧

*M*idlife crisis is that moment when you
realize your children and your clothes
are about the same age.
Bill Tammeus

❧

*F*amiliarity breeds contempt—and children.
Mark Twain

Genealogies

*Thus there were fourteen generations
in all from Abraham to David,
fourteen from David to the exile to Babylon,
and fourteen from the exile to the Christ.*
Matthew 1:17 NIV

❧

Noble and common blood is of the same color.
German Proverb

❧

*Parents who wonder where the younger generation
is going should remember where it came from.*
Sam Ewing

❧

*Ancestry is most important to those
who have done nothing themselves.*
Louis L'Amour

You can't expect to make a place in the sun
for yourself if you keep taking refuge
under the family tree.
Claude McDonald

Before most people start boasting
about their family tree,
they usually do a good pruning job.
O. A. Battista

The man who has nothing to boast of
but his illustrious ancestry, is like the potato—
the best part under ground.
Thomas Overbury

I don't know who my grandfather was;
I am much more concerned to know
what his grandson will be.
Abraham Lincoln

Marriage

*Therefore shall a man
leave his father and his mother,
and shall cleave unto his wife:
and they shall be one flesh.*

Genesis 2:24 KJV

❧

*Even if marriages are made in heaven,
man has to be responsible for the maintenance.*

James C. Dobson

❧

*Making marriage work is like running a farm.
You have to start all over again each morning.*

Anonymous

❧

*The Christian is supposed to love his neighbor,
and since his wife is his nearest neighbor,
she should be his deepest love.*

Martin Luther

A successful marriage requires falling in love
many times, always with the same person.
Mignon McLaughlin

❧

*M*ore marriages might survive if the partners
realized that sometimes the better
comes after the worse.
Doug Larson

❧

*M*arriage is like twirling a baton,
turning handsprings, or eating with chopsticks;
it looks so easy till you try it.
Helen Rowland

❧

*T*he exercise that really changes your life
is walking down the aisle.
Mary Ellen Pinkham

❧

*M*arriage is like a 7-Eleven. Not much variety,
but at 3 a.m., it's always there.
Anonymous

I guess walking slow getting married
is because it gives you
time to maybe change your mind.

Virginia Cary Hudson

❧

*B*efore marriage, a man will lie awake all night
thinking about something you said;
after marriage, he'll fall asleep before you
finish saying it.

Helen Rowland

❧

*B*y all means marry; if you get a good wife,
you'll become happy; if you get a bad one,
you'll become a philosopher.

Socrates

❧

*W*hy does a woman work ten years
to change a man's habits and then complain
that he's not the man she married?

Barbra Streisand

*M*arriage is a mutual admiration society
in which one person is always right,
and the other is always the husband.
Mary Martin

❧

Never go to bed mad. Stay up and fight.
Phyllis Diller

❧

A married couple that plays cards together
is just a fight that hasn't started yet.
George Burns

❧

*M*arried men live longer than single men,
but married men are a lot more willing to die.
Johnny Carson

❧

*M*arriage is a great institution,
but I'm not ready for an institution.
Mae West

Sexual Concerns

The husband should fulfill his marital duty
to his wife, and likewise the wife to her husband.
The wife's body does not belong to her alone
but also to her husband. In the same way,
the husband's body does not belong to him alone
but also to his wife.

1 Corinthians 7:3-4 NIV

The Bible has a word to describe "safe" sex:
It's called marriage.

Gary Smalley and John Trent

A kiss can be a comma, a question mark
or an exclamation point. That's basic spelling
that every woman ought to know.

Mistinguett

If homosexuality were the normal way,
God would have made Adam and Bruce.

Anita Bryant

A sex symbol becomes a thing.
I hate being a thing.
Marilyn Monroe

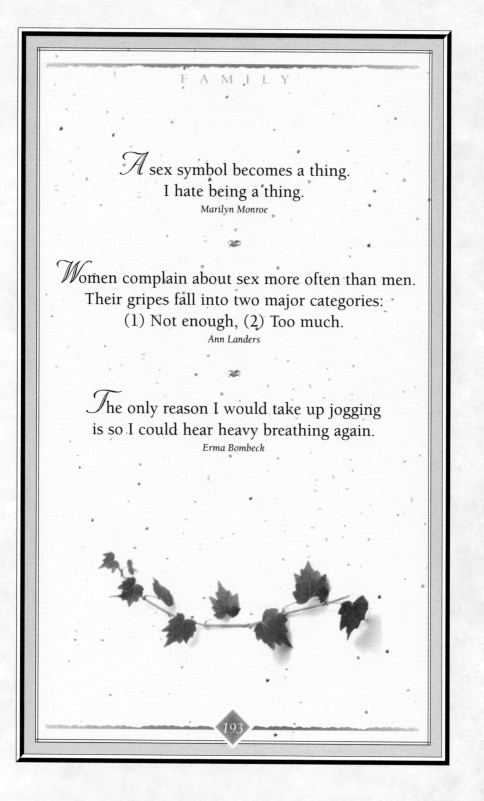

*W*omen complain about sex more often than men.
Their gripes fall into two major categories:
(1) Not enough, (2) Too much.
Ann Landers

*T*he only reason I would take up jogging
is so I could hear heavy breathing again.
Erma Bombeck

Children

Children are a gift from God;
they are his reward. Children
born to a young man are like sharp arrows
to defend him. Happy is the man
who has his quiver full of them....
Psalm 127:3-5 TLB

Life is a flame that is always burning itself out,
but it catches fire again every time a child is born.
George Bernard Shaw

A child can ask a thousand questions
that the wisest man cannot answer.
Jacob Abbott

Children have never been very good
at listening to their elders,
but they have never failed to imitate them.
James Baldwin

A **baby**

IS GOD'S

opinion *THAT*

THE *world*

should go

on.

❧ ❧ ❧

Carl Sandburg

*C*hildren have more need of models
than of critics.
French Proverb

❧

*T*here are no illegitimate children—
only illegitimate parents.
Leon R. Yankwich

❧

*Y*outh is, after all, just a moment,
but it is the moment, the spark that you
always carry in your heart.
Raisa M. Gorbachev

❧

I am not young enough to know everything.
Oscar Wilde

❧

*T*here is only one pretty child in the world,
and every mother has it.
Chinese Proverb

You don't have to suffer to be a poet.
Adolescence is enough suffering for anyone.
John Ciardi

❧

Teen-agers were put on earth to keep adults
from wasting time on the telephone.
Anonymous

❧

Children often hold a marriage together—
by keeping their parents too busy to quarrel
with each other.
Anonymous

❧

Any child can tell you
that the sole purpose of a middle name
is so he can tell when he's really in trouble.
Dennis Fakes

❧

Cleaning your house while your kids
are still growing is like shoveling the walk
before it stops snowing.
Phyllis Diller

Parenthood

*T*rain up a child in the way he should go:
and when he is old, he will not depart from it.

Proverbs 22:6 KJV

❧

*W*hen you are a mother,
you are never really alone in your thoughts.
A mother always has to think twice,
once for herself and once for her child.

Sophia Loren

❧

*M*aking the decision to have a child—
it's momentous. It is to decide forever to have
your heart go walking around outside your body.

Elizabeth Stone

❧

*The greatest thing a father can do for his children
is to love their mother.*

Josh McDowell

*C*ould I climb to the highest place in Athens,
I would lift my voice and proclaim—fellow-citizens,
why do ye turn and scrape every stone to gather
wealth, and take so little care of your children,
to whom one day you must relinquish it all?

Socrates

❧

*B*iology is the least of what
makes someone a mother.

Oprah Winfrey

❧

*P*arents of young children should realize
that few people, and maybe no one,
will find their children as enchanting as they do.

Barbara Walters

❧

*I*f you want your children to keep their feet
on the ground, put some responsibility
on their shoulders.

Abilgail Van Buren

❧

*T*here are many ways to measure success;
not the least of which is the way your child
describes you when talking to a friend.

Anonymous

*Fatherhood is pretending the present you
love most is soap-on-a-rope.*

Bill Cosby

⚬

*When I was a boy of fourteen, my father
was so ignorant I could hardly stand to have the
old man around. But when I got to be twenty-one,
I was astonished at how much he had learned
in seven years.*

Mark Twain

⚬

*In general my children refused to eat anything
that hadn't danced on TV.*

Erma Bombeck

⚬

*When I was a kid, my parents moved a lot—
but I always found them.*

Rodney Dangerfield

⚬

*I always wondered about where
"kingdom come" might be, since my mother
threatened so many times to knock me there.*

Bill Cosby

*B*y wisdom a house is built,
and through understanding it is established;
through knowledge its rooms are filled
with rare and beautiful treasures.
Proverbs 24:3-4 NIV

❧

*And if a house be divided against itself,
that house cannot stand.*
Mark 3:25 KJV

❧

*H*ome is the place where,
when you have to go there,
they have to take you in.
Robert Frost

❧

*I*t takes a heap o' livin' in a house
t' make it home.
Edgar A. Guest

A house without love may be a castle,
or a palace, but it is not a home....
John Lubbock

❧

*W*here is home? Home is where the heart
can laugh without shyness. Home is where the
heart's tears can dry at their own pace.
Vernon G. Baker

❧

*W*hen you finally go back to your old hometown,
you find it wasn't the old home
you missed but your childhood.
Sam Ewing

❧

A man travels the world over in search
of what he needs and returns home to find it.
George Moore

Though it rain gold and silver in a foreign land
and daggers and spears at home,
yet it is better to be at home.
Malay Proverb

Mid pleasures and palaces though we may roam,
Be it ever so humble,
there's no place like home.
John Howard Payne

When home is ruled according to God's Word,
angels might be asked to stay with us,
and they would not find themselves
out of their element.
Charles Spurgeon

Adultery

Can a man hold fire against his chest and not
be burned? Can he walk on hot coals and not
blister his feet? So it is with the man who commits
adultery with another's wife. He shall not go
unpunished for this sin.

Proverbs 6:27-29 TLB

⁂

How many homes are broken because of men
and women who are unfaithful! What sin
is committed every day at this point.
God will not hold you guiltless!

Billy Graham

⁂

The Bible says that thou shalt not commit adultery.
Moses got that law from God. It's a good law...
because back in those Bible days, if a man could
have six wives, three hundred concubines and
still commit adultery, I'd kill him myself.

Ray Charles

Fornication

*F*lee from sexual immorality.
All other sins a man commits are outside his body,
but he who sins sexually sins against his own body.
1 Corinthians 6:18 NIV

❧

*S*amson, for all his strong body, had a weak head,
or he would not have laid it in a harlot's lap.
Benjamin Franklin

❧

*T*here are few people who are not ashamed of
their love affairs when the infatuation is over.
François Duc de La Rochefoucauld

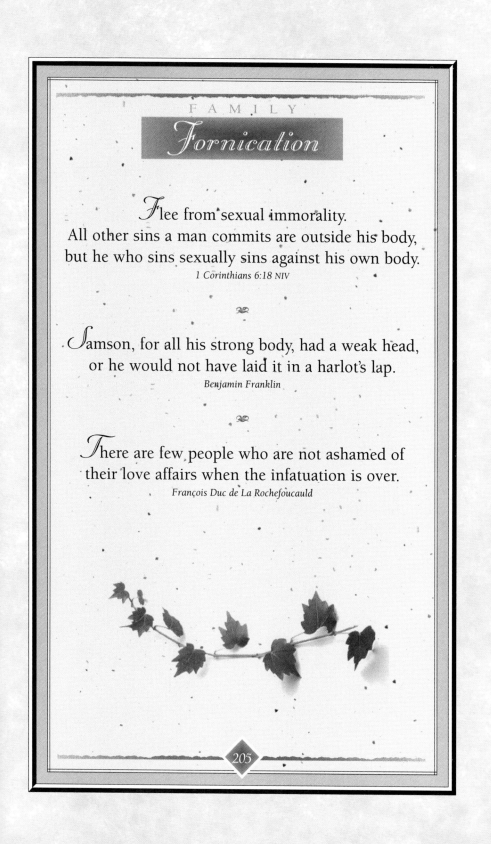

Divorce

"*I* hate divorce," says the LORD God of Israel....
Malachi 2:16 NIV

*H*owever often marriage is dissolved, it remains
indissoluble. Real divorce, the divorce of heart
and nerve and fiber, does not exist,
since there is no divorce from memory.
Virgilia Peterson

*T*here is something much worse
than living with a mate in disharmony.
It's living with God in disobedience.
Charles R. Swindoll

*S*o many persons who think divorce
a panacea for every ill find out, when they try it,
that the remedy is worse than the disease.
Dorothy Dix

*E*verybody says they'll marry till death,
and they're divorced a few weeks later.
I've lied to the judge twice myself.
Muhammad Ali

*A*limony is like putting gas into another guy's car.
Milton Berle

*I*f one falls down,
his friend can help him up.
But pity the man who falls
and has no one to help him up!
Ecclesiastes 4:10 NIV

❧

Friends are family you choose for yourself.
Jane Adams

❧

*Y*ou can make more friends in two months
by becoming more interested in other people
than you can in two years
by trying to get people interested in you.
Dale Carnegie

❧

I have room for one more friend,
and he is everyman.
Woody Guthrie

The best mirror is an old friend.

George Herbert

❧

A loyal friend laughs at your jokes
when they're not so good,
and sympathizes with your problems
when they're not so bad.

Arnold H. Glasow

❧

Friends are lost by calling often and calling seldom.

Scottish Proverb

❧

If you want an accounting of your worth,
count your friends.

Merry Browne

❧

Friends are those rare people
who ask how we are
and then wait to hear the answer.

Ed Cunningham

A friend hears the song in my heart
and sings it to me when my memory fails.
Anonymous

*Y*ou don't need to be a friend to everyone.
Remember the model of Jesus.
He preached to, ministered to,
and healed thousands of people,
but he only had twelve disciples.
Jim Conway

It takes a long time to grow an old friend.
John Leonard

*L*ots of people want to ride with you in the limo,
but what you want is someone
who will take the bus with you
when the limo breaks down.
Oprah Winfrey

*D*o not use a hatchet to remove a fly
from your friend's forehead.
Chinese Proverb

Relationships

Don't urge me to leave you or to turn back
from you. Where you go I will go, and where you
stay I will stay. Your people will be my people and
your God my God. Where you die I will die,
and there I will be buried. May the LORD deal
with me, be it ever so severely, if anything but
death separates you and me.

Ruth 1:16-17 NIV

❧

And one standing alone can be attacked
and defeated, but two can stand back-to-back
and conquer; three is even better,
for a triple-braided cord is not easily broken.

Ecclesiastes 4:12 TLB

❧

If I had a single flower
for every time I think about you,
I could walk forever in my garden.

Claudia Grandi

❧

'Tis better to be alone, than in bad company.

George Washington

*Why can't we build orphanages next to homes
for the aged? If someone's sitting in a rocker,
it won't be long before a kid will be in his lap.*
Cloris Leachman

❧

*Not many sounds in life...
exceed in interest a knock at the door.*
Charles Lamb

❧

*We agree completely on everything,
including the fact that we don't see eye to eye.*
Henry Kissinger and Golda Meir

❧

He liked to like people, therefore people liked him.
Mark Twain

❧

*There are two types of people—
those who come into a room and say,
"Well, here I am!"
and those who come in and say,
"Ah, there you are."*
Frederick L. Collins

*W*ell, enough about me. Let's talk about you.
What do you think about me?
Bette Midler

❧

*W*e had a lot in common,
I loved him and he loved him.
Shelley Winters

❧

*T*act is the art of making guests feel at home
when that's really where you wish they were.
George E. Bergman

❧

I only like two kinds of men:
domestic and foreign.
Mae West

❧

If you think it's hard to meet new people,
try picking up the wrong golf ball.
Jack Lemmon

If I'm

SUCH A

Legend,

THEN WHY

AM I **SO**

lonely?

❧ ❧ ❧

Judy Garland

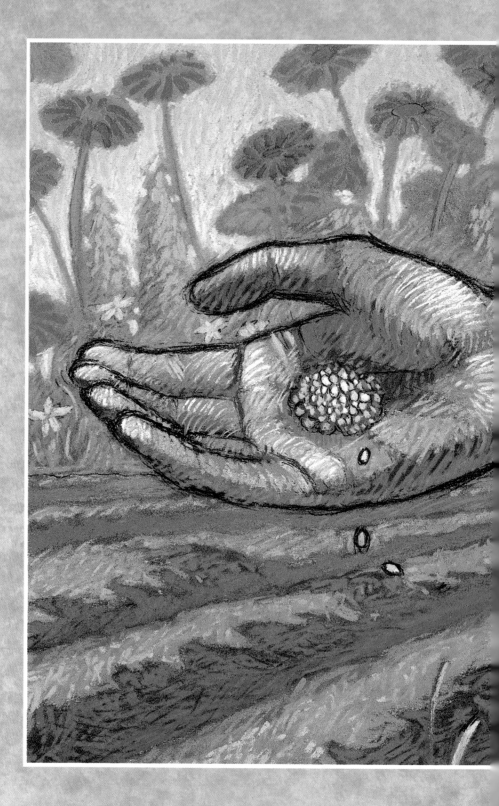

Witnessing

CHAPTER NINE

Will You Take the Witness Stand, Please?

❦ ❦ ❦

I never knew my palms could sweat so much. And the hard, wooden seat continued to grow even harder by the second. My heart was pounding so strongly against my chest that I just knew the others in the courtroom could hear it, too!

Why Lord? Why is this happening to me? You know it wasn't me. I'm innocent. Please, somebody, help me! Tell them I'm innocent. Surely a witness will come forward and save my life.

Some great books and movies through the years have been able to capture the value of WITNESSING to what we know.

Now is the time for us to stand up and be a witness—to tell the truth, the whole truth, and nothing but the truth. The Gospel must be told. And even beyond our words, our whole lifestyle can...

Be a lifesaving witness.

It is
better
to light
one *small*
CANDLE THAN
to **curse** the
darkness.

Confucius

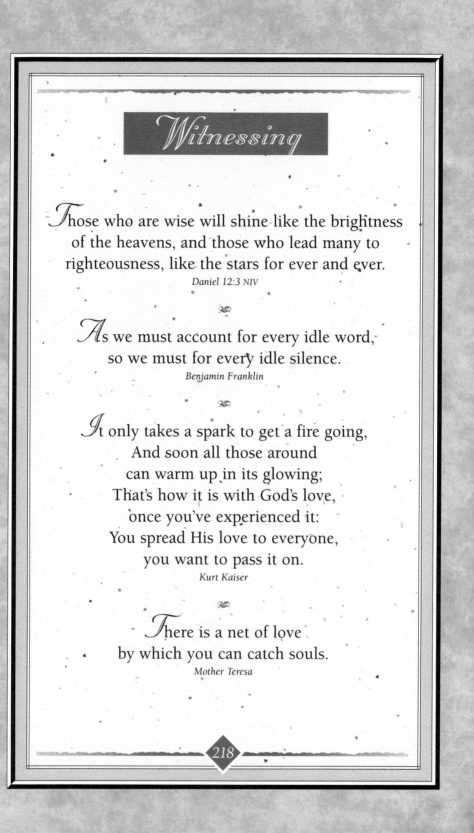

Witnessing

*T*hose who are wise will shine like the brightness
of the heavens, and those who lead many to
righteousness, like the stars for ever and ever.
Daniel 12:3 NIV

*A*s we must account for every idle word,
so we must for every idle silence.
Benjamin Franklin

*I*t only takes a spark to get a fire going,
And soon all those around
can warm up in its glowing;
That's how it is with God's love,
once you've experienced it:
You spread His love to everyone,
you want to pass it on.
Kurt Kaiser

*T*here is a net of love
by which you can catch souls.
Mother Teresa

*G*o ye therefore, and teach all nations, baptizing
them in the name of the Father, and of the Son,
and of the Holy Ghost: Teaching them to observe
all things whatsoever I have commanded you....

Matthew 28:19-20 KJV

*E*ducation's purpose is to replace an empty mind
with an open one.

Malcolm S. Forbes

*T*he mediocre teacher tells.
The good teacher explains.
The superior teacher demonstrates.
The great teacher inspires.

William Arthur Ward

To teach is to learn.

Japanese Proverb

*T*he teacher who is attempting to teach
without inspiring the pupil with a desire to learn
is hammering on cold iron.

Horace Mann

Experience is the teacher of fools.
Latin Proverb

❧

People want to know how much you care
before they care how much you know.
James F. Hind

❧

One thought driven home
is better than three left on base.
James Liter

❧

Education is learning what you
didn't even know you didn't know.
Daniel J. Boorstin

❧

I'm thirty years old,
but I read at the thirty-four-year-old level.
Dana Carvey

Good
TEACHERS
are *costly,*
BUT BAD
TEACHERS
cost more.

❧ ❧ ❧

Bob Talbert

Counseling

Plans fail for lack of counsel,
but with many advisers they succeed.
Proverbs 15:22 NIV

❧

In giving advice I advise you, be short.
Horace

❧

If you want to get rid of somebody
just tell 'em something for their own good.
Frank McKinney Hubbard

❧

The word "listen" contains the same letters
as the word "silent."
Alfred Brendel

❧

He who builds to every man's advice
will have a crooked house.
Danish Proverb

*W*hen we are well,
it is easy to give good advice to the sick.
* Terence

❧

*Y*ou don't need to take a person's advice
to make him feel good—just ask for it.
Laurence J. Peter

❧

*T*o attempt to advise conceited people
is like whistling against the wind.
Thomas Hood

❧

Talk low, talk slow, and don't say too much.
John Wayne

❧

*I*f it's free, it's advice; if you pay for it,
it's counseling; if you can use either one,
it's a miracle.
Jack Adams

❧

*T*alking about the advice he gives George Brett
on hitting, manager Jim Frey said, "I tell him,
'Attaway to hit, George.'"

Questioning

*D*o you know how God controls the clouds
and makes his lightning flash?
Job 37:15 NIV

❧

*Y*ou see things; and you say, "Why?"
But I dream things that never were;
and I say, "Why not?"
George Bernard Shaw

❧

*S*ometimes when we ask God our Why questions,
instead of giving us answers he gives us himself....
Mary Jane Worden

❧

*I*t is better to debate a question without settling it
than to settle a question without debating it.
Joseph Joubert

❧

*W*hile science may help explain how a virus
multiplies, it leaves unanswered why a tear is shed.
Bernard Lown

❧

*B*etter to ask twice than to lose your way once.
Danish Proverb

I'll give you a definitive maybe.

Samuel Goldwyn

❧

Hypothetical questions get hypothetical answers.

Joan Baez

❧

If it doesn't matter if you win or lose,
but how you play the game, why do we keep score?

Charley Boswell

❧

Question authority, but raise your hand first.

Bob Thaves

❧

There's nothing people like better than being asked
an easy question. For some reason, we're flattered
when a stranger asks us where Maple Street is in
our hometown and we can tell him.

Andrew A. Rooney

❧

Have you ever noticed that mice
don't have shoulders?

George Carlin

225

Instruction

*G*ive instruction to a wise man, and he
will be yet wiser: teach a just man,
and he will increase in learning.

Proverbs 9:9 KJV

A word to the wise is sufficient.

Plautus

*T*he man who does not read good books
has no advantage over the man who can't read.

Mark Twain

You ain't learnin' nothin' when you're talkin'.

Lyndon B. Johnson

*W*hen you straddle a thing
it takes a long time to explain it.

Will Rogers

*G*ive your brain as much attention as you do your
hair and you'll be a thousand times better off.

Malcolm X

*Y*ou can't always go by expert opinion.
A turkey, if you ask a turkey, should be stuffed
with grasshoppers, grit and worms.

Anonymous

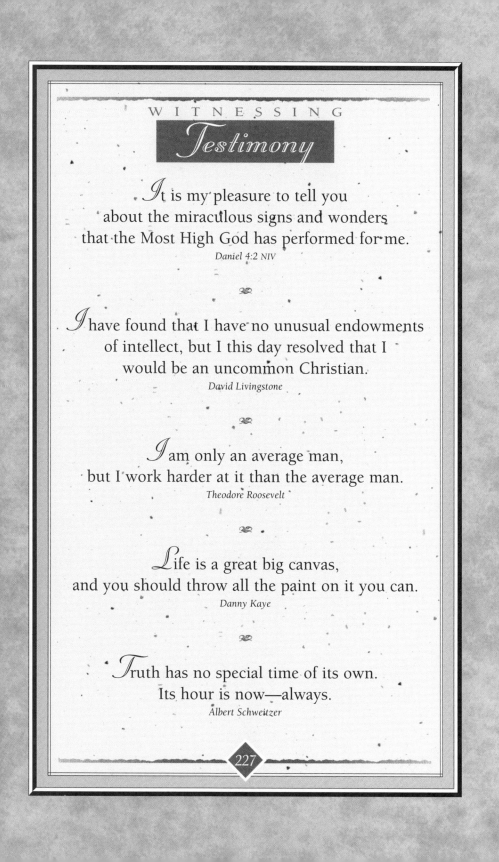

Testimony

*I*t is my pleasure to tell you
about the miraculous signs and wonders
that the Most High God has performed for me.

Daniel 4:2 NIV

I have found that I have no unusual endowments
of intellect, but I this day resolved that I
would be an uncommon Christian.

David Livingstone

I am only an average man,
but I work harder at it than the average man.

Theodore Roosevelt

*L*ife is a great big canvas,
and you should throw all the paint on it you can.

Danny Kaye

*T*ruth has no special time of its own.
Its hour is now—always.

Albert Schweitzer

227

Ministry

My children, don't neglect your duties any longer,
for the Lord has chosen you to minister to him....
2 Chronicles 29:11 TLB

❧

When you have a heart for God you have a heart
for ministry. The two go hand in hand.
Jill Briscoe

❧

Be thou the rainbow to the storms of life!
George Gordon Byron

❧

The goal of the missionary is to do God's will,
not to be useful or to win the lost. A missionary
is useful and he does win the lost, but that is not his
goal. His goal is to do the will of his Lord.
Oswald Chambers

❧

Wesley was once asked how he got the crowds.
He replied, "I set myself on fire, and the people
come to see me burn."
Maxwell Droke

How shall they hear without a preacher?
And how shall they preach,
except they be sent? as it is written,
How beautiful are the feet of them
that preach the gospel of peace,
and bring glad tidings of good things!

Romans 10:14-15 KJV

❧

My grand point in preaching
is to break the hard heart,
and to heal the broken one.

John Newton

❧

It is no use walking anywhere to preach
unless we preach as we walk.

St. Francis of Assisi

*I*f we had more hell in the pulpit,
we would have less hell in the pew.
Billy Graham

❧

*T*o love to preach is one thing—
to love those to whom we preach, quite another.
Richard Cecil

❧

*O*ne man practicing sportsmanship
is far better than 50 preaching it.
Knute Rockne

❧

A good sermon helps people in two ways.
Some rise from it greatly strengthened,
others wake from it refreshed.
E. C. McKenzie

Evangelism

*P*lead with the Lord of the harvest
to send out more laborers to help you, for the
harvest is so plentiful and the workers so few.

Luke 10:2 TLB

*Y*ou can't go on heavenly missions
without heavenly fire.

D. L. Moody

*L*ord, send me anywhere, only go with me.
Lay any burden on me, only sustain me.
Sever any tie but the tie that binds me to Thyself.

David Livingstone

I look upon the world as my parish.

John Wesley

*Y*our love has a broken wing
if it cannot fly across the sea.

Malthie D. Babcock

Gospel

For I am not ashamed of the gospel of Christ:
for it is the power of God
unto salvation to every one that believeth....
Romans 1:16 KJV

God writes the gospel not in the Bible alone,
but on trees, and flowers, and clouds, and stars.
Martin Luther

Did you ever notice that while the gospel
sets before us a higher and more blessed heaven
than any other religion, its hell
is also deeper and darker than any other?
Samuel Warren

Doctrine

You must teach what is in accord
with sound doctrine.

Titus 2:1 NIV

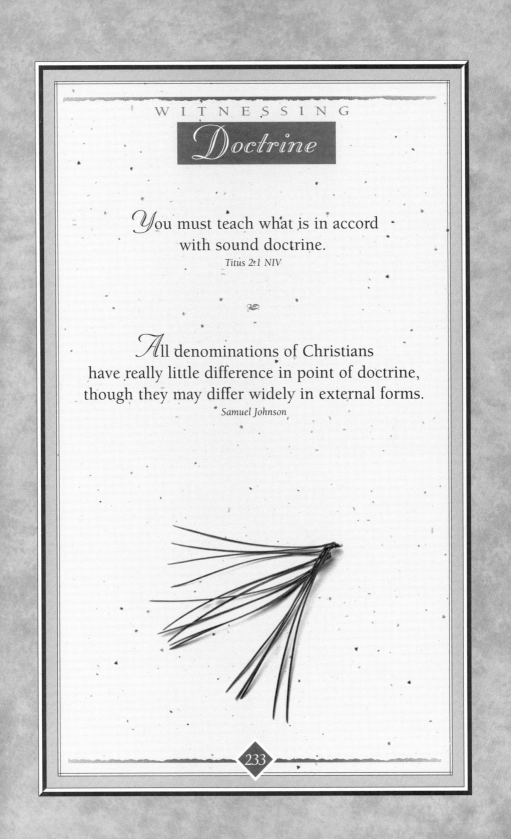

All denominations of Christians
have really little difference in point of doctrine,
though they may differ widely in external forms.

Samuel Johnson

Sayings

A word aptly spoken
is like apples of gold in settings of silver.
Proverbs 25:11 NIV

❧

A spoken word is not a sparrow.
Once it flies out, you can't catch it.
Russian Proverb

❧

*W*hen you were born, you cried and the world
rejoiced. Live your life in such a manner
that when you die the world cries and you rejoice.
Old Indian Saying

❧

*I*f it is the truth what does it matter who says it.
Anonymous

❧

Common sense is very uncommon.
Horace Greely

Be careful of your thoughts;
they may become words at any moment.
Iara Gassen

❧

Experience is what you get
when you don't get what you want.
Dan Stanford

❧

Three may keep a secret, if two of them are dead.
Benjamin Franklin

❧

Lead your life so you wouldn't be ashamed
to sell the family parrot to the town gossip.
Will Rogers

❧

I found out that it's not good to talk about my
troubles. Eighty percent of the people who hear
them don't care and the other twenty percent
are glad you're having trouble.
Tommy Lasorda

❧

Why doesn't the fellow who says
"I'm no speechmaker" let it go at that
instead of giving a demonstration?
Frank McKinney Hubbard

Commandments

CHAPTER TEN

COMMANDMENTS OR SUGGESTIONS?

❧   ❧   ❧

When I was a kid, my dad really knew how to "lay down the law," whereas Mom could be a bit of a pushover. When Mom told us to do something, we took it merely as a suggestion since she believed in giving each of us kids two or three chances.

"Hey, kids, pick up the front yard."

"Yeah, sure, Mom. We'll get to it," which being interpreted meant, "If we hold off till later, maybe she'll forget about it."

But DAD... When Dad told us to do something, we took it as law. The command had been issued, and consequences were immediate. We got to work or we got in big trouble!

"Kids, go sweep out the garage," he told us one lazy Saturday morning. (The floor was covered with sawdust and nails where my brothers and I had been "building" things.)

"Sure, Dad. We'll get to it."

"I mean *now*," he'd say. And we did it...*now*.

Actually, Mom and Dad both knew that it was only through chores and responsibilities that we could grow into reliable young adults. They had to teach us to obey their commands for our own good. (And to keep us from stepping on nails!)

You know, we're *God's* children, too. When He tells us through His Word to do something, we need to do it *now* so that we will become the mature Christians He would have us to be. If we don't, we'll face His consequences. After all...

God's commandments are not just suggestions!

Commandments

And this is his commandment,
That we should believe on the name
of his Son Jesus Christ, and love one another,
as he gave us commandment.

1 John 3:23 KJV

❧

Whoever wrote the Ten Commandments
made 'em short. They may not always be kept
but they can be understood.

Will Rogers

❧

A confirmation student was asked to list
the Ten Commandments in any order.
He wrote: "3, 6, 1, 8, 4, 5, 9, 2, 10, 7."

Anonymous

❧

If the Ten Commandments were not written
by Moses, then they were written
by another fellow of the same name.

Mark Twain

Offerings

*E*ach man should give what he
has decided in his heart to give,
not reluctantly or under compulsion,
for God loves a cheerful giver.

2 Corinthians 9:7 NIV

❧

*W*e cannot serve God and mammon;
but we can serve God with mammon.

Robert E. Speer

❧

As the purse is emptied the heart is filled.

Victor Hugo

❧

*D*o not give, as many rich men do,
like a hen that lays her egg and then cackles.

Henry Ward Beecher

❧

*T*he last place a person gets converted
is in the pocketbook.

Anonymous

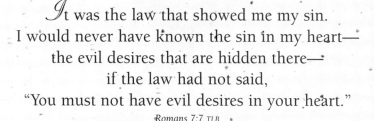

Law

$\mathcal{I}$t was the law that showed me my sin.
I would never have known the sin in my heart—
the evil desires that are hidden there—
if the law had not said,
"You must not have evil desires in your heart."
Romans 7:7 TLB

$\mathcal{N}$o man is above the law
and no man is below it;
nor do we ask any man's permission
when we require him to obey it.
Theodore Roosevelt

$\mathcal{M}$orality cannot be legislated,
but behavior can be regulated.
Judicial decrees may not change the heart,
but they can restrain the heartless.
Martin Luther King, Jr.

$\mathcal{P}$eople obey the law for one of two reasons:
they either love God or fear punishment.
Jack Kemp

Even thieves have a code of laws.
Cicero

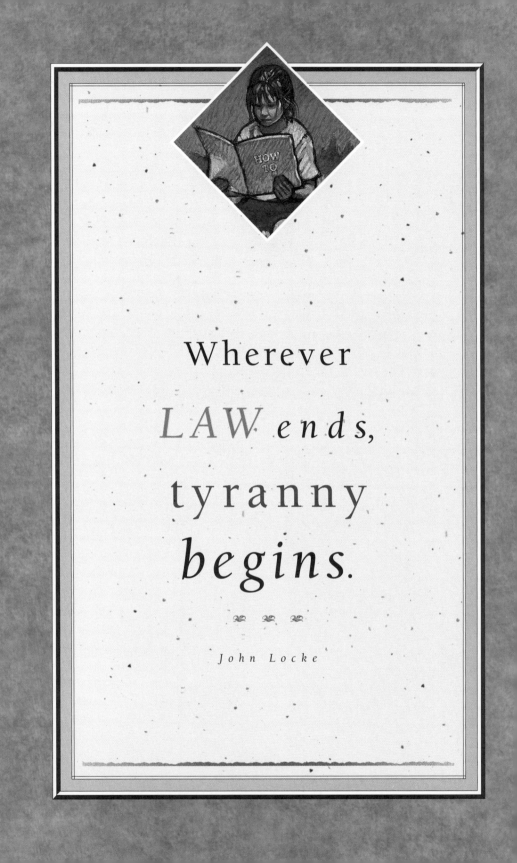

Wherever

LAW *ends,*

tyranny

begins.

☙ ☙ ☙

John Locke

*W*here is there any book of the law so clear
to each man as that written in his heart?
Leo N. Tolstoy

✦

*I*f you love the law and you love good sausage,
don't watch either of them being made.
Betty Talmadge

Priesthood

*E*very high priest is selected from among men
and is appointed to represent them
in matters related to God....
Hebrews 5:1 NIV

✦

A congregation which can't afford
to pay a clergyman enough want a missionary
more than they do a clergyman.
Josh Billings

Feasts

*T*hese are my appointed feasts,
the appointed feasts of the LORD,
which you are to proclaim as sacred assemblies.
Leviticus 23:2 NIV

Sabbath

*R*emember to observe the Sabbath as a holy day.
Six days a week are for your daily duties
and your regular work, but the seventh day
is a day of Sabbath rest before the Lord your God.
On that day you are to do no work of any kind....

Exodus 20:8-10 TLB

❧

I feel as if God had, by giving the Sabbath,
given fifty-two springs in every year.

Samuel Taylor Coleridge

❧

*S*unday is the golden clasp
that binds together the volume of the week.

Henry Wadsworth Longfellow

❧

*T*here are many persons who look on Sunday
as a sponge to wipe out the sins of the week.

Henry Ward Beecher

❧

*J*esus spoke about the ox in the ditch on the
Sabbath. But if your ox gets in the ditch every
Sabbath, you should either get rid of the ox
or fill up the ditch.

Billy Graham

Tithing

Will a man rob God? Surely not! And yet you
have robbed me. "What do you mean?
When did we ever rob you?" You have robbed me
of the tithes and offerings due to me.

Malachi 3:8 TLB

❧

When we tithe, God's blessing upon the
nine-tenths helps it to go further than the
ten-tenths without His blessing.

Billy Graham

❧

Some people will bring to church
a hymn book or a prayer book—
but not a pocket book.

Jack Herbert

❧

You cannot outgive God.

Billy Graham

Baptism

Confessing their sins,
they were baptized by him
in the Jordan River.

Matthew 3:6 NIV

Lord's Supper

*F*or every time you eat this bread
and drink this cup you are retelling the message
of the Lord's death, that he has died for you.
Do this until he comes again.

1 Corinthians 11:26 TLB

Church

*L*et us not neglect our church meetings,
as some people do, but encourage and warn
each other, especially now that the day of
his coming back again is drawing near.

Hebrews 10:25 TLB

*T*he blood of the martyrs
is the seed of the church.

St. Jerome

I never weary of great churches.
It is my favourite kind of mountain scenery.
Mankind was never so happily inspired
as when it made a cathedral.

Robert Louis Stevenson

A

CHURCH

is *God*

BETWEEN

four walls.

French Proverb

Church growth has come to refer more
to such things as location, marketing, architecture,
programs, and head counts than to the
maturity of the body of Christ.

Charles Colson

❧

*The Church after all is not a club of saints;
it is a hospital for sinners.*

George Craig Stewart

❧

Don't stay away from church
because there are so many hypocrites.
There's always room for one more.

Arthur R. Adams

❧

Going to church doesn't make you a Christian
any more than going to a garage
makes you an automobile.

Billy Sunday

❧

I always find that statistics are hard to swallow
and impossible to digest. The only one I can
ever remember is that if all the people who go to
sleep in church were laid end to end they would
be a lot more comfortable.

Mrs. Robert A. Taft

Deacon

*D*eacons, likewise, are to be men
worthy of respect, sincere, not indulging in much
wine, and not pursuing dishonest gain:

1 Timothy 3:8 NIV

Growth

*M*eanwhile, the church had peace
throughout Judea, Galilee and Samaria,
and grew in strength and numbers. The believers
learned how to walk in the fear of the Lord
and in the comfort of the Holy Spirit.

Acts 9:31 TLB

*W*e find comfort among those
who agree with us—
growth among those who don't.

Frank A. Clark

Growth is the only evidence of life.

John Henry Newman

I may be old but I haven't stopped growing!

Oliver Wendell Holmes, Jr.

History

CHAPTER ELEVEN

62 Home Runs for Hughey!

❧ ❧ ❧

"Mantle, Maris, Mays, Aaron, and Ruth will now need to make room for the newest addition to baseball's elite: Hughey!"

Great headlines! And what a way to enter the HISTORY books!

For many, such aspirations to make history for themselves (or their children) begin with that preschool soccer team, that first piano practice, and yes, even that initial base hit on the tee ball field.

History—that old silver fox which has gone before us and which in time will go on after us. What legacy, what renown, what meaning could be more valuable to our years on this earth than that our names be entered in the only HISTORY book that really matters...

The Book of Life (Revelation 21:27)

History

*T*hen Goliath, a Philistine champion from Gath,
came out of the Philistine ranks to face
the forces of Israel. He was a giant of a man,
measuring over nine feet tall!
1 Samuel 17:4 TLB

❧

*A*bove his head they placed the written charge
against him: THIS IS JESUS, THE KING OF THE JEWS.
Matthew 27:37 NIV

❧

*H*istory is but the unrolled scroll of prophecy.
James A. Garfield

❧

*T*hose who cannot remember the past
are condemned to repeat it.
George Santayana

❧

*Y*ou can clutch the past so tightly to your chest that
it leaves your arms too full to embrace the present.
Jan Glidewell

❧

*C*hrist is the great central fact in the world's history;
to him everything looks forward or backward.
All the lines of history converge upon him.
Charles Spurgeon

HISTORY

Of course, it's the same old story.
Truth usually is the same old story.
Margaret Thatcher

❧

*H*istory is His story.
Anonymous

❧

*Yesterday's gone on down the river,
and you can't get it back.*
Larry McMurtry

❧

If you believe the past can't be changed,
you haven't read a celebrity's autobiography.
Sam Ewing

❧

*H*e who does not remember the past
is condemned to forget where he parked.
Anonymous

❧

*D*on't look back.
Something may be gaining on you.
Satchel Paige

Creation

*I*n the beginning God created the heaven and the earth.
Genesis 1:1 KJV

❧

*N*ature is the art of God.
Dante

❧

*T*he miracles of nature do not seem miracles
because they are so common.
If no one had ever seen a flower, even a dandelion
would be the most startling event in the world.
Anonymous

❧

*P*oems are made by fools like me,
But only God can make a tree.
Joyce Kilmer

❧

Behind every flower stands God.
Japanese Proverb

❧

*G*od doesn't have to put his name on a label
in the corner of a meadow
because nobody else makes meadows.
Cecil Laird

❧

*G*od wisely designed the human body
so that we can neither pat our own backs
nor kick ourselves too easily.
Anonymous

255

War

All the days of Saul there was bitter war
with the Philistines, and whenever Saul saw a mighty
or brave man, he took him into his service.

1 Samuel 14:52 NIV

To save your world you asked this man to die;
Would this man, could he see you now, ask why?

W. H. Auden

In a civil war the firing line is invisible;
it passes through the hearts of men.

Antoine de Saint-Exupéry

Mankind must put an end to war
or war will put an end to mankind.

John F. Kennedy

*In the final choice a soldier's pack
is not so heavy a burden as a prisoner's chains.*

Dwight D. Eisenhower

There will be no veterans of World War III.

Walter Mondale

In time of war the devil makes more room in hell.

German Proverb

HISTORY

Oh God, let this horrible war quickly come
to an end that we may all return home
and engage in the only work that is worthwhile—
and that is the salvation of men.

Thomas Jonathan "Stonewall" Jackson

✻

In war there is no second prize for the runner-up.

Omar Bradley

✻

Can anything be more ridiculous
than that a man should have the right to kill me
because he lives on the other side of the water,
and because his ruler has a quarrel with mine,
though I have none with him?

Blaise Pascal

✻

You know you can be killed just as dead
in an unjustified war, as you can
in one protecting your own home.

Will Rogers

✻

Praise the Lord and pass the ammunition.

Howell M. Forgy

✻

Do not needlessly endanger your lives
until I give you the signal.

Dwight D. Eisenhower

*I*n the six hundredth year of Noah's life,
on the seventeenth day of the second month—
on that day all the springs of the great deep
burst forth, and the floodgates of the heavens
were opened. And rain fell on the earth
forty days and forty nights.

Genesis 7:11-12 NIV

*I*t was the third hour when they crucified him....
At the sixth hour darkness came over the whole land
until the ninth hour.

Mark 15:25, 33 NIV

*W*hat is time? The shadow on the dial,
the striking of the clock, the running of the sand,
day and night, summer and winter, months,
years, centuries—these are but the arbitrary
and outward signs—the measure of time,
not time itself. Time is the life of the soul.

Henry Wadsworth Longfellow

*N*o hand can make the clock
strike for me the hours that are passed.

George Gordon Byron

Time and tide wait for no man.
Geoffrey Chaucer

❧

*L*ost, yesterday, somewhere between sunrise
and sunset, two golden hours, each set
with sixty diamond minutes.
No reward is offered, for they are gone forever!
Lydia H. Sigourney

❧

*A*n inch of gold cannot buy an inch of time.
Chinese Proverb

❧

*L*ife is not dated merely by years.
Events are sometimes the best calendars.
Benjamin Disraeli

❧

*T*IME IS
Too Slow for those who Wait,
Too Swift for those who Fear,
Too Long for those who Grieve,
Too Short for those who Rejoice,
But for those who Love,
Time is Eternity.
Henry Van Dyke

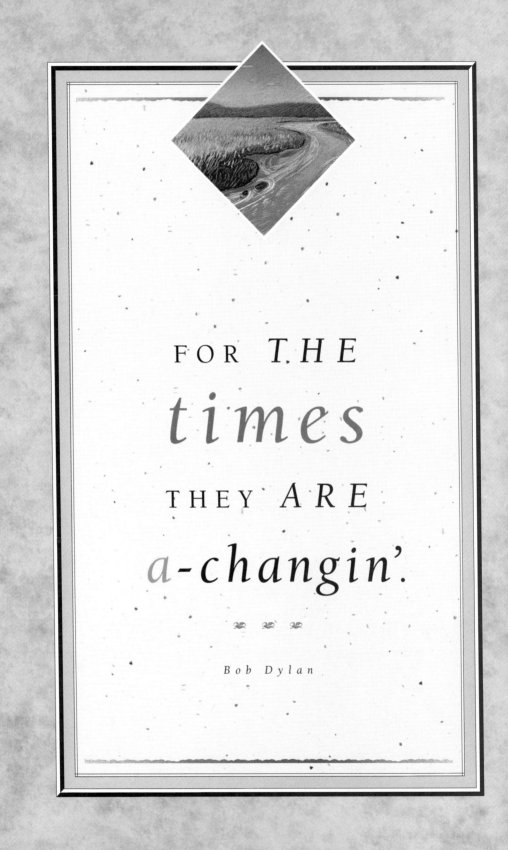

FOR *THE*

times

THEY *ARE*

a-changin'.

❧ ❧ ❧

Bob Dylan

H I S T O R Y

*T*ime is but the stream I go a-fishing in.
Henry David Thoreau

❧

*S*pring is God's way of saying, "One more time!"
Robert Orben

❧

*T*omorrow is the day when idlers work, and fools
reform, and mortal men lay hold on heaven.
Edward Young

❧

*I*n times like these, it helps to recall
that there have always been times like these.
Paul Harvey

❧

*A*ll my possessions for a moment of time.
Queen Elizabeth I (Last Words)

❧

I've been on a calendar, but never on time.
Marilyn Monroe

❧

*T*hree o'clock is always too late or too early
for anything you want to do.
Jean-Paul Sartre

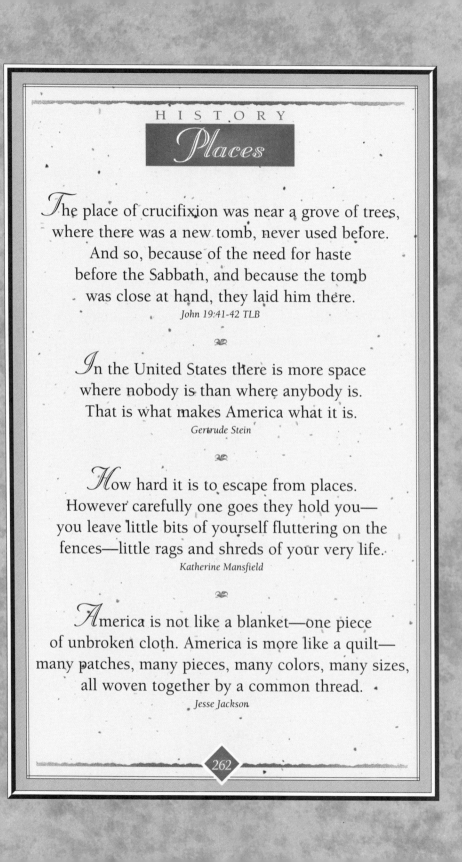

Places

*T*he place of crucifixion was near a grove of trees,
where there was a new tomb, never used before.
And so, because of the need for haste
before the Sabbath, and because the tomb
was close at hand, they laid him there.

John 19:41-42 TLB

*I*n the United States there is more space
where nobody is than where anybody is.
That is what makes America what it is.

Gertrude Stein

*H*ow hard it is to escape from places.
However carefully one goes they hold you—
you leave little bits of yourself fluttering on the
fences—little rags and shreds of your very life.

Katherine Mansfield

*A*merica is not like a blanket—one piece
of unbroken cloth. America is more like a quilt—
many patches, many pieces, many colors, many sizes,
all woven together by a common thread.

Jesse Jackson

God made the country, and man made the town.
William Cowper

❧

*A place is yours when you
know where all the roads go.*
Anonymous

❧

From the mountains to the prairies,
To the oceans white with foam,
God bless America,
My home sweet home!
Irving Berlin

❧

Patriotism is your conviction that this country
is superior to all other countries
because you were born in it.
George Bernard Shaw

❧

An American is a guy who sips Brazilian
coffee from an English cup while sitting on
Danish furniture after coming home in his German
car from an Italian movie—and then writes his
Congressman with a Japanese ball point pen,
demanding that he do something about all the
gold that's leaving the country.
Harry Lieberman

Journeys

*E*veryone was required to return to his ancestral home for this registration. And because Joseph was a member of the royal line, he had to go to Bethlehem in Judea, King David's ancient home—journeying there from the Galilean village of Nazareth. He took with him Mary, his fiancée....

Luke 2:3-5 TLB

*T*he journey of a thousand miles begins with one step.

Lao-Tse

*E*verywhere is walking distance if you have the time.

Steven Wright

*I*f all difficulties were known at the outset of a long journey, most of us would never start out at all.

Dan Rather

*F*ar away is far away only if you don't go there.
Anonymous

※

*T*here are no shortcuts to any place worth going.
Beverly Sills

※

I always love to begin a journey
on Sundays, because I shall have the prayers
of the church to preserve all that travel by land,
or by water.
Jonathan Swift

※

*E*veryone journeys through character
as well as through time. The person one becomes
depends on the person one has been.
Dick Francis

※

A journey of 1000 miles begins
with a single delay of two hours before takeoff.
Anonymous

※

*N*ever take a cross-country car trip with a kid
who has just learned to whistle.
Jean Deuel

Narration

*T*he manna was like coriander seed
and looked like resin. The people went around
gathering it, and then ground it in a handmill
or crushed it in a mortar. They cooked it in a pot
or made it into cakes. And it tasted like
something made with olive oil.

Numbers 11:7-8 NIV

*E*very man's life is a fairy-tale
written by God's fingers.

Hans Christian Andersen

Chronological Record of Events

*A*s for the events of King David's reign,
from beginning to end,
they are written in the records...
together with the details of his reign and power....

1 Chronicles 29:29-30 NIV

*E*verything that happens in the world is part
of a great plan of God running through all time.

Henry Ward Beecher

The historian is the prophet looking backward.

Carter G. Woodson

❧

Statistics always remind me of the fellow
who drowned in a river whose average depth
was only three feet.

Woody Hayes

❧

Just once I'd like to see the win-loss records
of doctors right out front where people
could see them—won ten, lost three, tied two.

Abe Lemons

Vocations

As Jesus walked beside the Sea of Galilee,
he saw Simon and his brother Andrew casting a net
into the lake, for they were fishermen.

Mark 1:16 NIV

❧

Choose a job you love and you
will never have to work a day in your life.

Confucius

❧

It is not what a man does that determines whether
his work is sacred or secular, it is why he does it.

A. W. Tozer

267

If a man is called to be a streetsweeper, he should sweep streets even as Michelangelo painted, or Beethoven composed music, or Shakespeare wrote poetry. He should sweep streets so well that all the hosts of heaven and earth will pause to say, here lived a great streetsweeper who did his job well.

Martin Luther King, Jr.

❧

To fulfill a dream, to be allowed to sweat over lonely labor, to be given a chance to create, is the meat and potatoes of life. The money is the gravy.

Bette Davis

❧

Work spares us from three great evils: boredom, vice, and need.

Voltaire

❧

God gives every bird its food, but he does not throw it into the nest.

J. G. Holland

❧

Don't tell me how hard you work. Tell me how much you get done.

James Ling

The world is full of willing people;
some willing to work, the rest willing to let them.

Robert Frost

❧

People who make a living doing something
they don't enjoy wouldn't even be happy
with a one-day work week.

Edward "Duke" Ellington

❧

The only thing that ever sat its way to success
was a hen.

Sarah Brown

❧

The person who knows "how"
will always have a job. The person who knows
"why" will always be his boss.

Diane Ravitch

❧

By working faithfully eight hours a day,
you may eventually get to be a boss
and work twelve hours a day.

Robert Frost

❧

Accomplishing the impossible means only that
the boss will add it to your regular duties.

Doug Larson

Kings

*A*nd he took their king's crown from off his head,
the weight whereof was a talent of gold with the
precious stones: and it was set on David's head....
2 Samuel 12:30 KJV

❧

Uneasy lies the head that wears a crown.
William Shakespeare

❧

*B*etter have as king a vulture advised by swans
than a swan advised by vultures.
Panchatantra

❧

A leader is a dealer in hope.
Napoleon Bonaparte

❧

I am more afraid of an army of 100 sheep
led by a lion than an army of 100 lions
led by a sheep.
Talleyrand

If you can talk with crowds and keep your virtue,
Or walk with Kings—nor lose the common touch...
Yours is the Earth and everything that's in it,
And—which is more—you'll be a Man, my son!

Rudyard Kipling

❧

Many a politician who's been appointed
acts as if he's been anointed.

Evan Esar

❧

Life is like a dog-sled team.
If you ain't the lead dog,
the scenery never changes.

Lewis Grizzard

❧

In a few years there will be only five kings
in the world—the King of England
and the four kings in a pack of cards.

King Farouk I

Earth

*T*hus the heavens and the earth
were completed in all their vast array.
Genesis 2:1 NIV

❧

*E*arth's crammed with heaven,
And every common bush afire with God.
Elizabeth Barrett Browning

❧

*S*ummer ends and autumn comes,
and he who would have it otherwise
would have high tide always
and a full moon every night.
Hal Borland

❧

O world, I cannot hold thee close enough!
Edna St. Vincent Millay

❧

*E*arth, with her thousand voices, praises God.
Samuel Taylor Coleridge

*T*he sun does not rise because of the rotation
of the earth. The sun rises because God
says to it, "Get up."

G. K. Chesterton

❧

*S*unshine is delicious, rain is refreshing,
wind braces up, snow is exhilarating;
there is no such thing as bad weather,
only different kinds of good weather.

John Ruskin

❧

*T*he Rainbow comes and goes,
And lovely is the Rose.

William Wordsworth

❧

*T*here is nothing in which the birds
differ more from man than the way in which they
can build and yet leave a landscape as it was before.

Robert Lynd

❧

*O*ne of the worst mistakes you can make
as a gardener is to think you're in charge.

Janet Gillespie

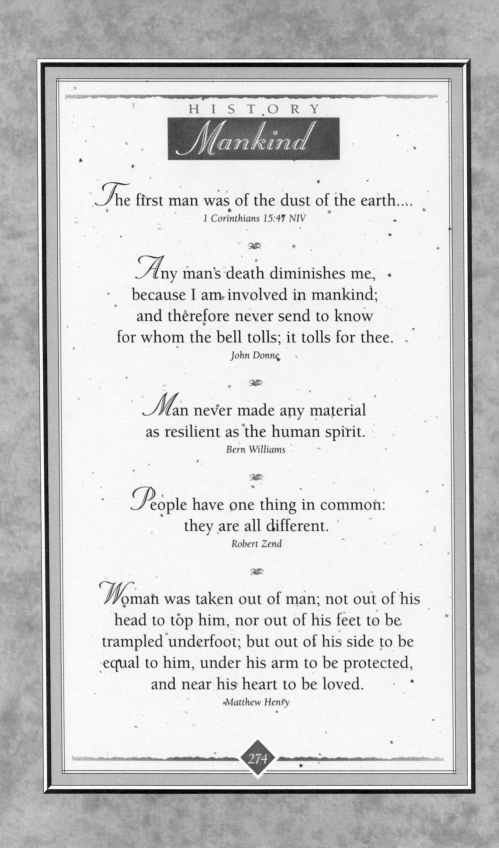

*T*he first man was of the dust of the earth....
1 Corinthians 15:47 NIV

*A*ny man's death diminishes me,
because I am involved in mankind;
and therefore never send to know
for whom the bell tolls; it tolls for thee.
John Donne

*M*an never made any material
as resilient as the human spirit.
Bern Williams

*P*eople have one thing in common:
they are all different.
Robert Zend

*W*oman was taken out of man; not out of his
head to top him, nor out of his feet to be
trampled underfoot; but out of his side to be
equal to him, under his arm to be protected,
and near his heart to be loved.
Matthew Henry

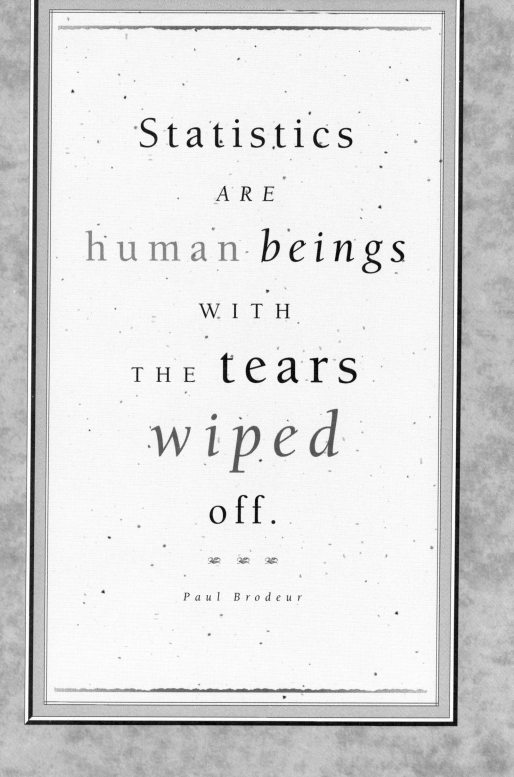

Statistics ARE human beings WITH THE tears wiped off.

Paul Brodeur

*A*ristotle, on being censured for giving alms
to a bad man, answered:
"I did not give it to the man,
I gave it to humanity."

❧

*T*here are three classes of men—
lovers of wisdom, lovers of honor, lovers of gain.
Plato

❧

*L*et each man think himself an act of God,
His mind a thought, his life a breath of God.
Philip James Bailey

❧

*M*an is the only animal that blushes. Or needs to.
Mark Twain

Common-looking people are the best in the world;
that is the reason the Lord makes so many of them.
Abraham Lincoln

Some people march to a different drummer—
and some people polka.
Anonymous

Men don't care what's on TV.
They only care what else is on TV.
Jerry Seinfeld

Man was created on the sixth day so that he
could not be boastful, since he came after the flea
in the order of creation.
Haggadah

It's human nature to keep doing something
as long as it's pleasurable and you can succeed at it—
which is why the world population
continues to double every 40 years.
Peter Lynch

Prophecy

CHAPTER TWELVE

WHAT'S UP AHEAD?

❧ ❧ ❧

"PLAN FOR A DAY OF ADVENTURE!" "TAKE A RIDE FOR THE THRILL OF YOUR LIFE!" "FUN AND FOOD AHEAD!"

Signs along the highway were beckoning us to the amusement park with promises of great things. And my friends and I were ready!

When we arrived at the park, lines were already winding and twisting well out from the shaded walkways. Blistering heat or not, we were determined to take that notoriously "thrilling" roller-coaster ride. The clank of steel and clatter of cars as they headed up the treacherously steep track made us hold our breath in excitement. It was our turn!

As our car twisted and careened, hurtling forward, then sideways, then upside down, we screamed and laughed and thought we would fall out besides! It was unbelievably wild! The park was everything the signs had said it would be. What a day!

God's prophets are a lot like those signs posted along the highway. Throughout the Bible the prophets told of the promises of God. They revealed the blessings ahead for an obedient people, but warned of God's judgment of the rebellious. Those who heard and heeded were ready, not just for a day of adventure but...

An eternal adventure.

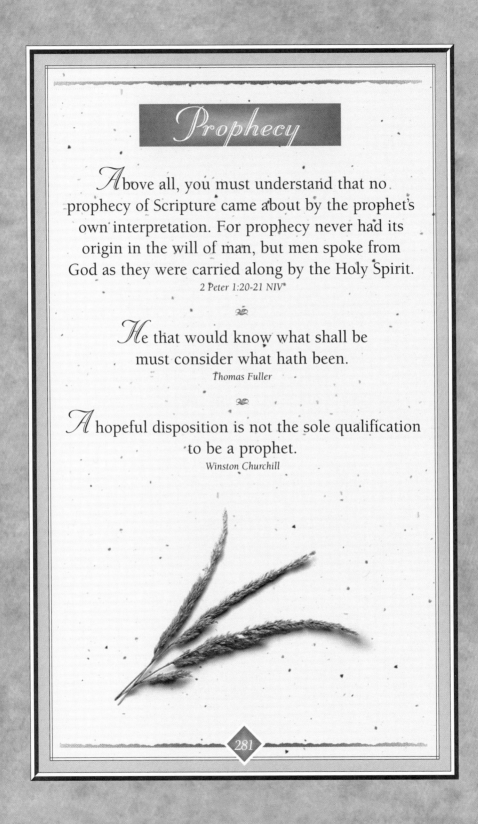

Prophecy

*A*bove all, you must understand that no
prophecy of Scripture came about by the prophet's
own interpretation. For prophecy never had its
origin in the will of man, but men spoke from
God as they were carried along by the Holy Spirit.

2 Peter 1:20-21 NIV

*H*e that would know what shall be
must consider what hath been.

Thomas Fuller

A hopeful disposition is not the sole qualification
to be a prophet.

Winston Churchill

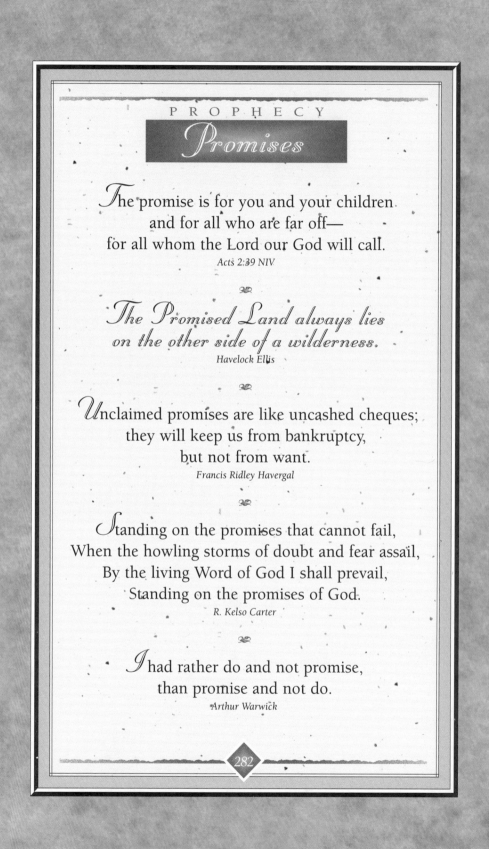

Promises

*T*he promise is for you and your children
and for all who are far off—
for all whom the Lord our God will call.
Acts 2:39 NIV

❧

*The Promised Land always lies
on the other side of a wilderness.*
Havelock Ellis

❧

*U*nclaimed promises are like uncashed cheques;
they will keep us from bankruptcy,
but not from want.
Francis Ridley Havergal

❧

*S*tanding on the promises that cannot fail,
When the howling storms of doubt and fear assail,
By the living Word of God I shall prevail,
Standing on the promises of God.
R. Kelso Carter

❧

I had rather do and not promise,
than promise and not do.
Arthur Warwick

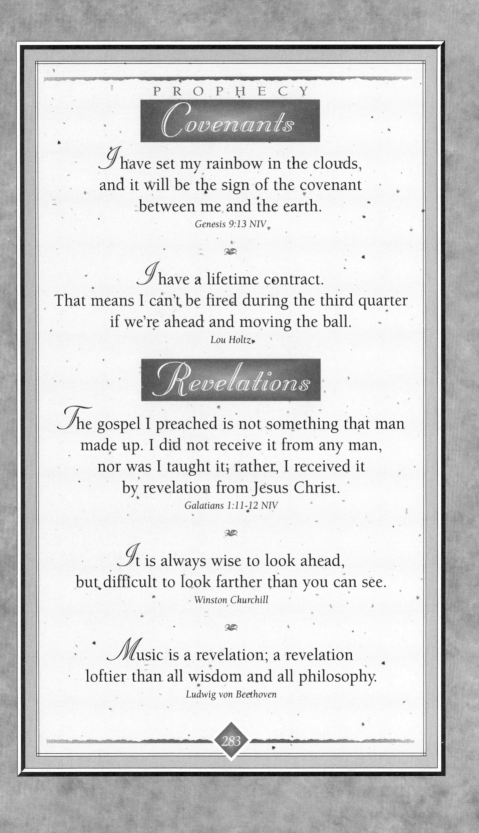

PROPHECY

Covenants

I have set my rainbow in the clouds,
and it will be the sign of the covenant
between me and the earth.

Genesis 9:13 NIV

I have a lifetime contract.
That means I can't be fired during the third quarter
if we're ahead and moving the ball.

Lou Holtz

Revelations

*T*he gospel I preached is not something that man
made up. I did not receive it from any man,
nor was I taught it; rather, I received it
by revelation from Jesus Christ.

Galatians 1:11-12 NIV

*I*t is always wise to look ahead,
but difficult to look farther than you can see.

Winston Churchill

*M*usic is a revelation; a revelation
loftier than all wisdom and all philosophy.

Ludwig von Beethoven

Vows

If a man vow a vow unto the LORD...
he shall not break his word, he shall do
according to all that proceedeth out of his mouth.

Numbers 30:2 KJV

❧

To make a vow for life is to make oneself a slave.

Voltaire

❧

None are so fond of secrets as those
who do not mean to keep them.

Caleb C. Colton

Visions

In the visions I saw while lying in my bed, I looked,
and there before me was a messenger, a holy one,
coming down from heaven.

Daniel 4:13 NIV

❧

A rock pile ceases to be a rock pile
the moment a single man contemplates it,
bearing within him the image of a cathedral.

Antoine de Saint-Exupéry

The very essence of leadership is that you have to
have a vision. You can't blow an uncertain trumpet.
Theodore Hesburgh

❧

The vision must be followed by the venture.
It is not enough to stare up the steps—
we must step up the stairs.
Vance Havner

❧

It isn't that they can't see the solution.
It is that they can't see the problem.
G. K. Chesterton

❧

Vision is the art of seeing things invisible.
Jonathan Swift

❧

A glimpse is not a vision. But to a man on a
mountain road by night, a glimpse of the
next three feet of road may matter more
than a vision of the horizon.
C. S. Lewis

❧

Vision without work is visionary,
Work without vision is mercenary,
Vision and work together,
They are missionary.
Anonymous

Dreams

*A*nd he dreamed, and behold a ladder
set up on the earth, and the top of it
reached to heaven: and behold the angels of God
ascending and descending on it.
Genesis 28:12 KJV

❧

I have a dream my four little children
will one day live in a nation where they
will not be judged by the color of their skin
but by content of their character.
Martin Luther King, Jr.

❧

Saddle your dreams afore you ride 'em.
Mary Webb

❧

*I*t's a risky thing to talk about one's
most secret dreams a bit too early.
Tove Jansson

❧

*T*he poorest of all men
is not the man without a cent;
it is the man without a dream.
Anonymous

Goals

ARE

dreams

with

DEADLINES.

Diana Scharf Hunt

A child on a farm sees a plane
fly overhead and dreams of a faraway place.
A traveler on the plane sees the farmhouse...
and dreams of home.
Carl Burns

❧

*S*ometimes my dreams are so deep
that I dream that I'm dreaming.
Ray Charles

❧

*T*here are those who will say
that the liberation of humanity,
the freedom of man and mind,
is nothing but a dream.
They are right. It is the American dream.
Archibald MacLeish

❧

*W*e grow great by dreams.
All big men are dreamers.
Woodrow Wilson

PROPHECY

*G*od also bound himself with an oath,
so that those he promised to help would be
perfectly sure and never need to wonder
whether he might change his plans.

Hebrews 6:17 TLB

*I*t is not the oath that makes us believe the man,
but the man the oath.

Aeschylus

*A*fter describing himself in a court of law
as the greatest living actor,
George Arliss excused his boast with
"You see, I am on oath."

*T*he one who calls you is faithful and he will do it.

1 Thessalonians 5:24 NIV

*R*esolve to perform what you ought.
Perform without fail what you resolve.

Benjamin Franklin

Inspiration

Long ago God spoke in many different ways
to our fathers through the prophets [in visions,
dreams, and even face to face], telling them little
by little about his plans. But now in these days
he has spoken to us through his Son...:

Hebrews 1:1-2 TLB

※

Inspiration is a fragile thing...
just a breeze, touching the green foliage
of a city park, just a whisper from the soul
of a friend. Just a line of verse
clipped from some forgotten magazine...
Inspiration...who can say where it is born,
and why it leaves us?

Margaret Sangster

※

Two stonecutters were asked what they
were doing. The first said, "I'm cutting this stone
into blocks." The second replied,
"I'm on a team that's building a cathedral."

Anonymous

※

History celebrates few persons
who waited for inspiration.

Ned Arthur

And he came and dwelt in a city called Nazareth:
that it might be fulfilled which was spoken
by the prophets, He shall be called a Nazarene.

Matthew 2:23 KJV

❧

You are more than a human being,
you are a human becoming.

Og Mandino

❧

To live only for some future goal is shallow.
It's the sides of the mountain that sustain life,
not the top.

Robert M. Pirsig

❧

Nothing is or can be accidental with God.

Henry Wadsworth Longfellow

❧

Instead of always looking at the past,
I put myself ahead twenty years
and try to look at what I need to do
now in order to get there then.

Diana Ross

Future

*T*hen the angel said to me, "These words
are trustworthy and true: 'I am coming soon!'
God, who tells his prophets what the future holds,
has sent his angel to tell you this will happen soon...."
Revelation 22:6-7 TLB

❧

*N*o matter what a man's past may have been,
his future is spotless.
John R. Rice

❧

*I*f there were no future life,
our souls would not thirst for it.
Jean Paul Richter

❧

No one can walk backward into the future.
Joseph Hergesheimer

❧

*M*emories are the key not to the past,
but to the future.
Corrie ten Boom

When I
LOOK at the
future
IT'S SO BRIGHT
it BURNS my
eyes.

❧ ❧ ❧

Oprah Winfrey

When all else is lost, the future still remains.
Bovee

❧

The future is like heaven—
everyone exalts it
but no one wants to go there now.
James Baldwin

❧

Anticipating is even more fun than recollecting.
Malcolm S. Forbes

❧

Nobody gets to live life backward.
Look ahead—that's where your future lies.
Ann Landers

❧

I sometimes believe we're heading very fast
for Armageddon right now.
Ronald Reagan

*O*nly mothers can think of the future—
because they give birth to it in their children.
Maxim Gorky

❧

I went through life as a
"player to be named later."
Joe Garagiola

❧

The future ain't what it used to be.
Lawrence "Yogi" Berra

THE BOOK OF PROVERBS

The Book of Proverbs was written primarily by King Solomon in about 950 B.C., during what has commonly been referred to as the "Golden Age" of Israel. Since that time it has been considered by scholars and laymen alike to be the greatest and most inspiring book of wisdom ever published. For this reason it deserves its place in *A Rainbow of Hope.*

Following then is the Book of Proverbs in its entirety as it appears in *The NIV Rainbow Study Bible.*

—The Publisher

*God gave Solomon wisdom and very great insight,
and a breadth of understanding
as measureless as the sand on the seashore.*
1 KINGS 4:29 (NIV)

PROVERBS

Proverbs of Solomon: Attaining wisdom.

1 The proverbs of Solomon[a] son of David, king of Israel:[b]

[2]for attaining wisdom and discipline;
for understanding words of insight;
[3]for acquiring a disciplined and prudent life,
doing what is right and just and fair;
[4]for giving prudence to the simple,[c]
knowledge and discretion[d] to the young—
[5]let the wise listen and add to their learning,[e]
and let the discerning get guidance—
[6]for understanding proverbs and parables,[f]
the sayings and riddles[g] of the wise.

[7]The fear of the LORD[h] is the beginning of knowledge,
but fools[a] despise wisdom and discipline.

Warning against enticement of sinners.

[8]Listen, my son,[i] to your father's instruction
and do not forsake your mother's teaching.[j]
[9]They will be a garland to grace your head
and a chain to adorn your neck.[k]

[10]My son, if sinners entice[l] you,
do not give in[m] to them.[n]
[11]If they say, "Come along with us;
let's lie in wait[o] for someone's blood,
let's waylay some harmless soul;
[12]let's swallow them alive, like the grave,[b]
and whole, like those who go down to the pit;[p]
[13]we will get all sorts of valuable things
and fill our houses with plunder;
[14]throw in your lot with us,
and we will share a common purse"—
[15]my son, do not go along with them,
do not set foot[q] on their paths;[r]
[16]for their feet rush into sin,
they are swift to shed blood.[s]
[17]How useless to spread a net
in full view of all the birds!
[18]These men lie in wait for their own blood;
they waylay only themselves!
[19]Such is the end of all who go after ill-gotten gain;
it takes away the lives of those who get it.[t]

Warning against rejecting wisdom.

[20]Wisdom calls aloud[u] in the street,
she raises her voice in the public squares;
[21]at the head of the noisy streets[c] she cries out,
in the gateways of the city she makes her speech:

[22]"How long will you simple ones[d][v]
love your simple ways?
How long will mockers delight in mockery
and fools hate knowledge?
[23]If you had responded to my rebuke,
I would have poured out my heart to you
and made my thoughts known to you.
[24]But since you rejected me when I called[w]
and no one gave heed when I stretched out my hand,
[25]since you ignored all my advice
and would not accept my rebuke,
[26]I in turn will laugh[x] at your disaster;
I will mock when calamity overtakes you[y]—

1:1
[a]1Ki 4:29-34
[b]Pr 10:1;25:1;
Ecc 1:1

1:4
[c]Pr 8:5
[d]Pr 2:10-11;
8:12

1:5
[e]Pr 9:9

1:6
[f]Ps 49:4; 78:2
[g]Nu 12:8

1:7
[h]Job 28:28;
Ps 111:10;
Pr 9:10;
15:33;
Ecc 12:13

1:8
[i]Pr 4:1
[j]Pr 6:20

1:9
[k]Pr 4:1-9

1:10
[l]Ge 39:7
[m]Dt 13:8
[n]Pr 16:29;
Eph 5:11

1:11
[o]Ps 10:8

1:12
[p]Ps 28:1

1:15
[q]Ps 119:101
[r]Ps 1:1;
Pr 4:14

1:16
[s]Pr 6:18;
Isa 59:7

1:19
[t]Pr 15:27

1:20
[u]Pr 8:1;
9:1-3,13-15

1:22
[v]Pr 8:5;
9:4,16

1:24
[w]Isa 65:12;
66:4;
Jer 7:13;
Zec 7:11

1:26
[x]Ps 2:4
[y]Pr 6:15;
10:24

a7 The Hebrew words rendered *fool* in Proverbs, and often elsewhere in the Old Testament, denote one who is morally deficient.   b12 Hebrew *Sheol*
c21 Hebrew; Septuagint / *on the tops of the walls*
d22 The Hebrew word rendered *simple* in Proverbs generally denotes one without moral direction and inclined to evil.

27when calamity overtakes you like a
storm,
when disaster sweeps over you like
a whirlwind,
when distress and trouble
overwhelm you.
28"Then they will call to me but I will
not answer;*a*
they will look for me but will not
find me.*b*
29Since they hated knowledge
and did not choose to fear the
LORD,*c*
30since they would not accept my
advice
and spurned my rebuke,*d*
31they will eat the fruit of their ways
and be filled with the fruit of their
schemes.*e*
32For the waywardness of the simple
will kill them,
and the complacency of fools will
destroy them;*f*
33but whoever listens to me will live
in safety*g*
and be at ease, without fear of
harm."*h*

Wisdom for the upright.

2 My son, if you accept my words
and store up my commands
within you,
2turning your ear to wisdom
and applying your heart to
understanding,*i*
3and if you call out for insight
and cry aloud for understanding,
4and if you look for it as for silver
and search for it as for hidden
treasure,*j*
5then you will understand the fear of
the LORD
and find the knowledge of God.*k*
6For the LORD gives wisdom,*l*
and from his mouth come
knowledge and understanding.
7He holds victory in store for the
upright,
he is a shield*m* to those whose
walk is blameless,*n*
8for he guards the course of the just

1:28
*a*1Sa 8:18;
Isa 1:15;
Jer 11:11;
Mic 3:4
*b*Job 27:9;
Pr 8:17;
Eze 8:18;
Zec 7:13
1:29
*c*Job 21:14
1:30
*d*ver 25;
Ps 81:11
1:31
*e*Job 4:8;
Pr 14:14;
Isa 3:11;
Jer 6:19
1:32
*f*Jer 2:19
1:33
*g*Ps 25:12;
Pr 3:23
*h*Ps 112:8
2:2
*i*Pr 22:17
2:4
*j*Job 3:21;
Pr 3:14;
Mt 13:44
2:5
*k*Pr 1:7
2:6
*l*1Ki 3:9,12;
Jas 1:5
2:7
*m*Pr 30:5-6
*n*Ps 84:11
2:8
*o*1Sa 2:9;
Ps 66:9
2:10
*p*Pr 14:33
2:11
*q*Pr 4:6; 6:22
2:13
*r*Pr 4:19;
Jn 3:19
2:14
*s*Pr 10:23;
Jer 11:15
2:15
*t*Ps 125:5
*u*Pr 21:8
2:16
*v*Pr 5:1-6;
6:20-29;7:5-27
2:17
*w*Mal 2:14
2:18
*x*Pr 7:27
2:19
*y*Ecc 7:26
2:21
*z*Ps 37:29
2:22
*a*Job 18:17;
Ps 37:38

and protects the way of his faithful
ones.*o*
9Then you will understand what is
right and just
and fair—every good path.
10For wisdom will enter your heart,*p*
and knowledge will be pleasant to
your soul.
11Discretion will protect you,
and understanding will guard
you.*q*

12Wisdom will save you from the ways
of wicked men,
from men whose words are
perverse,
13who leave the straight paths
to walk in dark ways,*r*
14who delight in doing wrong
and rejoice in the perverseness of
evil,*s*
15whose paths are crooked*t*
and who are devious in their
ways.*u*

16It will save you also from the
adulteress,*v*
from the wayward wife with her
seductive words,
17who has left the partner of her youth
and ignored the covenant she
made before God.*e w*
18For her house leads down to death
and her paths to the spirits of the
dead.*x*
19None who go to her return
or attain the paths of life.*y*

20Thus you will walk in the ways of
good men
and keep to the paths of the
righteous.
21For the upright will live in the
land,*z*
and the blameless will remain in it;
22but the wicked will be cut off from
the land,*a*
and the unfaithful will be torn
from it.*b*

*b*Dt 28:63; Pr 10:30

e17 Or *covenant of her God*

Wisdom brings blessings.

3 My son, do not forget my
teaching,[a]
but keep my commands in your
heart,

[2] for they will prolong your life many
years[b]
and bring you prosperity.

[3] Let love and faithfulness never leave
you;
bind them around your neck,
write them on the tablet of your
heart.[c]
[4] Then you will win favor and a good
name
in the sight of God and man.[d]

[5] Trust in the LORD[e] with all your heart
and lean not on your own
understanding;
[6] in all your ways acknowledge him,
and he will make your paths[f]
straight.[†][g]

[7] Do not be wise in your own eyes;[h]
fear the LORD and shun evil.[i]
[8] This will bring health to your body[j]
and nourishment to your bones.[k]

[9] Honor the LORD with your wealth,
with the firstfruits[l] of all your
crops;
[10] then your barns will be filled[m] to
overflowing,
and your vats will brim over with
new wine.[n]

[11] My son, do not despise the LORD's
discipline[o]
and do not resent his rebuke,
[12] because the LORD disciplines those
he loves,[p]
as a father[g] the son he delights in.[q]

[13] Blessed is the man who finds
wisdom,
the man who gains understanding,
[14] for she is more profitable than silver
and yields better returns than
gold.[r]
[15] She is more precious than rubies;[s]
nothing you desire can compare
with her.[t]

[16] Long life is in her right hand;
in her left hand are riches and
honor.[u]
[17] Her ways are pleasant ways,
and all her paths are peace.[v]
[18] She is a tree of life[w] to those who
embrace her;
those who lay hold of her will be
blessed.

[19] By wisdom the LORD laid the earth's
foundations,[x]
by understanding he set the
heavens[y] in place;
[20] by his knowledge the deeps were
divided,
and the clouds let drop the dew.

[21] My son, preserve sound judgment
and discernment,
do not let them out of your sight;[z]
[22] they will be life for you,
an ornament to grace your neck.[a]
[23] Then you will go on your way in
safety,
and your foot will not stumble;[b]
[24] when you lie down,[c] you will not be
afraid;
when you lie down, your sleep[d]
will be sweet.
[25] Have no fear of sudden disaster
or of the ruin that overtakes the
wicked,
[26] for the LORD will be your confidence
and will keep your foot[e] from
being snared.

[27] Do not withhold good from those
who deserve it,
when it is in your power to act.
[28] Do not say to your neighbor,
"Come back later; I'll give it
tomorrow"—
when you now have it with you.[f]

[29] Do not plot harm against your
neighbor,
who lives trustfully near you.
[30] Do not accuse a man for no reason—
when he has done you no harm.

3:1
[a] Pr 4:5
3:2
[b] Pr 4:10
3:3
[c] Ex 13:9;
Pr 6:21; 7:3;
2Co 3:3
3:4
[d] 1Sa 2:26;
Lk 2:52
3:5
[e] Ps 37:3,5
3:6
[f] 1Ch 28:9
[g] Pr 16:3;
Isa 45:13
3:7
[h] Ro 12:16
[i] Job 1:1;
Pr 16:6
3:8
[j] Pr 4:22
[k] Job 21:24
3:9
[l] Ex 22:29;
23:19;
Dt 26:1-15
3:10
[m] Dt 28:8
[n] Joel 2:24
3:11
[o] Job 5:17
3:12
[p] Pr 13:24;
Rev 3:19
[q] Dt 8:5;
Heb 12:5-6*
3:14
[r] Job 28:15;
Pr 8:19;
16:16
3:15
[s] Job 28:18
[t] Pr 8:11
3:16
[u] Pr 8:18
3:17
[v] Pr 16:7;
Mt 11:28-30
3:18
[w] Ge 2:9;
Pr 11:30;
Rev 2:7
3:19
[x] Ps 104:24
[y] Pr 8:27-29
3:21
[z] Pr 4:20-22
3:22
[a] Pr 1:8-9
3:23
[b] Ps 37:24;
Pr 4:12
3:24
[c] Lev 26:6;
Ps 3:5
[d] Job 11:18

3:26[e] 1Sa 2:9 3:28[f] Lev 19:13; Dt 24:15

[†]6 Or *will direct your paths* [g]12 Hebrew;
Septuagint */ and he punishes*

31Do not envy[a] a violent man
　or choose any of his ways,
32for the LORD detests a perverse man[b]
　but takes the upright into his
　　confidence.[c]

33The LORD's curse[d] is on the house of
　the wicked,[e]
　but he blesses the home of the
　　righteous.[f]
34He mocks proud mockers
　but gives grace to the humble.[g]
35The wise inherit honor,
　but fools he holds up to shame.

*Fatherly advice on
the importance of wisdom.*

4 Listen, my sons,[h] to a father's
　instruction;
　pay attention and gain
　　understanding.
2I give you sound learning,
　so do not forsake my teaching.
3When I was a boy in my father's
　house,
　still tender, and an only child of my
　　mother,
4he taught me and said,
　"Lay hold of my words with all
　　your heart;
　keep my commands and you will
　　live.[i]
5Get wisdom,[j] get understanding;
　do not forget my words or swerve
　　from them.
6Do not forsake wisdom, and she will
　protect you;[k]
　love her, and she will watch over
　　you.
7Wisdom is supreme; therefore get
　wisdom.
　Though it cost all[l] you have,[h] get
　　understanding.[m]
8Esteem her, and she will exalt you;
　embrace her, and she will honor
　　you.[n]
9She will set a garland of grace on
　your head
　and present you with a crown of
　　splendor.[o]"

10Listen, my son, accept what I say,

3:31
[a]Ps 37:1;
Pr 24:1-2
3:32
[b]Pr 11:20
[c]Job 29:4;
Ps 25:14
3:33
[d]Dt 11:28;
Mal 2:2
[e]Zec 5:4
[f]Ps 1:3
3:34
[g]Jas 4:6*;
1Pe 5:5*
4:1
[h]Pr 1:8
4:4
[i]Pr 7:2
4:5
[j]Pr 16:16
4:6
[k]2Th 2:10
4:7
[l]Mt 13:44-46
[m]Pr 23:23
4:8
[n]1Sa 2:30;
Pr 3:18
4:9
[o]Pr 1:8-9
4:10
[p]Pr 3:2
4:11
[q]1Sa 12:23
4:12
[r]Job 18:7;
Pr 3:23
4:13
[s]Pr 3:22
4:14
[t]Ps 1:1;
Pr 1:15
4:16
[u]Ps 36:4;
Mic 2:1
4:18
[v]Isa 26:7
[w]2Sa 23:4;
Da 12:3;
Mt 5:14;
Php 2:15
4:19
[x]Job 18:5;
Pr 2:13;
Isa 59:9-10;
Jn 12:35
4:20
[y]Pr 5:1
4:21
[z]Pr 3:21;7:1-2
4:22
[a]Pr 3:8;
12:18
4:23
[b]Mt 12:34;
Lk 6:45

and the years of your life will be
　many.[p]
11I guide[q] you in the way of wisdom
　and lead you along straight paths.
12When you walk, your steps will not
　be hampered;
　when you run, you will not
　　stumble.[r]
13Hold on to instruction, do not let it go;
　guard it well, for it is your life.[s]
14Do not set foot on the path of the
　wicked
　or walk in the way of evil men.[t]
15Avoid it, do not travel on it;
　turn from it and go on your way.
16For they cannot sleep till they do
　evil;[u]
　they are robbed of slumber till they
　　make someone fall.
17They eat the bread of wickedness
　and drink the wine of violence.

18The path of the righteous[v] is like the
　first gleam of dawn,
　shining ever brighter till the full
　　light of day.[w]
19But the way of the wicked is like
　deep darkness;[x]
　they do not know what makes
　　them stumble.

20My son, pay attention to what I say;
　listen closely to my words.[y]
21Do not let them out of your sight,[z]
　keep them within your heart;
22for they are life to those who find
　them
　and health to a man's whole body.[a]
23Above all else, guard your heart,
　for it is the wellspring of life.[b]
24Put away perversity from your mouth;
　keep corrupt talk far from your lips.
25Let your eyes look straight ahead,
　fix your gaze directly before you.
26Make level[i] paths for your feet[c]
　and take only ways that are firm.
27Do not swerve to the right or the
　left;[d]
　keep your foot from evil.

4:26 [c]Heb 12:13* 4:27 [d]Dt 5:32; 28:14

h7 Or *Whatever else you get* i26 Or *Consider the*

Warning against adultery.

5 My son, pay attention to my wisdom,
　　listen well to my words[a] of insight,
[2]that you may maintain discretion
　　and your lips may preserve knowledge.
[3]For the lips of an adulteress drip honey,
　　and her speech is smoother than oil;[b]
[4]but in the end she is bitter as gall,[c]
　　sharp as a double-edged sword.
[5]Her feet go down to death;
　　her steps lead straight to the grave.[j][d]
[6]She gives no thought to the way of life;
　　her paths are crooked, but she knows it not.[e]

[7]Now then, my sons, listen[f] to me,
　　do not turn aside from what I say.
[8]Keep to a path far from her,[g]
　　do not go near the door of her house,
[9]lest you give your best strength to others
　　and your years to one who is cruel,
[10]lest strangers feast on your wealth
　　and your toil enrich another man's house.
[11]At the end of your life you will groan,
　　when your flesh and body are spent.
[12]You will say, "How I hated discipline!
　　How my heart spurned correction![h]
[13]I would not obey my teachers
　　or listen to my instructors.
[14]I have come to the brink of utter ruin
　　in the midst of the whole assembly."

[15]Drink water from your own cistern,
　　running water from your own well.
[16]Should your springs overflow in the streets,
　　your streams of water in the public squares?
[17]Let them be yours alone,
　　never to be shared with strangers.
[18]May your fountain[i] be blessed,
　　and may you rejoice in the wife of your youth.[j]
[19]A loving doe, a graceful deer[k]—
　　may her breasts satisfy you always,
　　may you ever be captivated by her love.
[20]Why be captivated, my son, by an adulteress?
　　Why embrace the bosom of another man's wife?

[21]For a man's ways are in full view[l] of the LORD,
　　and he examines all his paths.[m]
[22]The evil deeds of a wicked man ensnare him;[n]
　　the cords of his sin hold him fast.[o]
[23]He will die for lack of discipline,[p]
　　led astray by his own great folly.

Warning against laziness.

6 My son, if you have put up security for your neighbor,[q]
　　if you have struck hands in pledge[r] for another,
[2]if you have been trapped by what you said,
　　ensnared by the words of your mouth,
[3]then do this, my son, to free yourself,
　　since you have fallen into your neighbor's hands:
　Go and humble yourself;
　　press your plea with your neighbor!
[4]Allow no sleep to your eyes,
　　no slumber to your eyelids.[s]
[5]Free yourself, like a gazelle from the hand of the hunter,
　　like a bird from the snare of the fowler.[t]

[6]Go to the ant, you sluggard;[u]
　　consider its ways and be wise!
[7]It has no commander,
　　no overseer or ruler,
[8]yet it stores its provisions in summer
　　and gathers its food at harvest.[v]

Cross references (center column)

5:1
[a]Pr 4:20; 22:17

5:3
[b]Ps 55:21; Pr 2:16; 7:5

5:4
[c]Ecc 7:26

5:5
[d]Pr 7:26-27

5:6
[e]Pr 30:20

5:7
[f]Pr 7:24

5:8
[g]Pr 7:1-27

5:12
[h]Pr 1:29; 12:1

5:18
[i]SS 4:12-15
[j]Ecc 9:9; Mal 2:14

5:19
[k]SS 2:9; 4:5

5:21
[l]Ps 119:168; Hos 7:2
[m]Job 14:16; Job 31:4; 34:21; Pr 15:3; Jer 16:17; 32:19; Heb 4:13

5:22
[n]Ps 9:16
[o]Nu 32:23; Ps 7:15-16; Pr 1:31-32

5:23
[p]Job 4:21; 36:12

6:1
[q]Pr 17:18
[r]Pr 11:15; 22:26-27

6:4
[s]Ps 132:4

6:5
[t]Ps 91:3

6:6
[u]Pr 20:4

6:8
[v]Pr 10:4

j5 Hebrew *Sheol*

⁹How long will you lie there, you
  sluggard?ᵃ
When will you get up from your
  sleep?
¹⁰A little sleep, a little slumber,
  a little folding of the hands to
    restᵇ—
¹¹and povertyᶜ will come on you like a
    bandit
  and scarcity like an armed man.ᵏ

¹²A scoundrel and villain,
  who goes about with a corrupt
    mouth,
¹³ who winks with his eye,ᵈ
  signals with his feet
  and motions with his fingers,
¹⁴ who plots evilᵉ with deceit in his
    heart—
  he always stirs up dissension.ᶠ
¹⁵Therefore disaster will overtake him
    in an instant;
  he will suddenly be
    destroyed—without remedy.ᵍ

Seven things hated by the LORD.

¹⁶There are six things the LORD hates,
  seven that are detestable to him:
¹⁷   haughty eyes,
    a lying tongue,ʰ
    hands that shed innocent blood,ⁱ
¹⁸   a heart that devises wicked
      schemes,
    feet that are quick to rush into
      evil,ʲ
¹⁹   a false witnessᵏ who pours out
      lies
    and a man who stirs up
      dissension among brothers.ˡ

Further warning against adultery.

²⁰My son, keep your father's
    commands
  and do not forsake your mother's
    teaching.ᵐ
²¹Bind them upon your heart forever;
  fasten them around your neck.ⁿ
²²When you walk, they will guide you;
  when you sleep, they will watch
    over you;
  when you awake, they will speak
    to you.

6:9
ᵃPr 24:30-34

6:10
ᵇPr 24:33

6:11
ᶜPr 24:30-34

6:13
ᵈPs 35:19

6:14
ᵉMic 2:1
ᶠver 16-19

6:15
ᵍ2Ch 36:16

6:17
ʰPs 120:2;
Pr 12:22
ⁱDt 19:10;
Isa 1:15; 59:7

6:18
ʲGe 6:5

6:19
ᵏPs 27:12
ˡver 12-15

6:20
ᵐPr 1:8

6:21
ⁿPr 3:3; 7:1-3

6:23
ᵒPs 19:8;
119:105

6:24
ᵖPr 2:16; 7:5

6:26
ᑫPr 7:22-23;
29:3

6:29
ʳEx 20:14
ˢPr 2:16-19;
5:8

6:31
ᵗEx 22:1-14

6:32
ᵘEx 20:14
ᵛPr 7:7;
9:4,16

6:33
ʷPr 5:9-14

6:34
ˣNu 5:14
ʸGe 34:7

6:35
ᶻJob 31:9-11;
SS 8:7

7:1
ᵃPr 1:8; 2:1

²³For these commands are a lamp,
  this teaching is a light,ᵒ
and the corrections of discipline
  are the way to life,
²⁴keeping you from the immoral
    woman,
  from the smooth tongue of the
    wayward wife.ᵖ
²⁵Do not lust in your heart after her
    beauty
  or let her captivate you with her
    eyes,
²⁶for the prostitute reduces you to a
    loaf of bread,
  and the adulteress preys upon your
    very life.ᑫ
²⁷Can a man scoop fire into his lap
  without his clothes being burned?
²⁸Can a man walk on hot coals
  without his feet being scorched?
²⁹So is he who sleepsʳ with another
    man's wife;ˢ
  no one who touches her will go
    unpunished.

³⁰Men do not despise a thief if he steals
    to satisfy his hunger when he is
    starving.
³¹Yet if he is caught, he must pay
    sevenfold,ᵗ
  though it costs him all the wealth
    of his house.
³²But a man who commits adultery ᵘ
    lacks judgment;ᵛ
  whoever does so destroys himself.
³³Blows and disgrace are his lot,
  and his shame will neverʷ be
    wiped away;
³⁴for jealousyˣ arouses a husband's
    fury,ʸ
  and he will show no mercy when
    he takes revenge.
³⁵He will not accept any compensation;
  he will refuse the bribe, however
    great it is.ᶻ

Warning against the adulteress.

7 My son,ᵃ keep my words
  and store up my commands
    within you.

ᵏ11 Or like a vagrant / and scarcity like a beggar

303

2 Keep my commands and you will
live;[a]
guard my teachings as the apple of
your eye.
3 Bind them on your fingers;
write them on the tablet of your
heart.[b]
4 Say to wisdom, "You are my sister,"
and call understanding your
kinsman;
5 they will keep you from the
adulteress,
from the wayward wife with her
seductive words.[c]

6 At the window of my house
I looked out through the lattice.
7 I saw among the simple,
I noticed among the young men,
a youth who lacked judgment.[d]
8 He was going down the street near
her corner,
walking along in the direction of
her house
9 at twilight,[e] as the day was fading,
as the dark of night set in.

10 Then out came a woman to meet
him,
dressed like a prostitute and with
crafty intent.
11 (She is loud[f] and defiant,
her feet never stay at home;
12 now in the street, now in the
squares,
at every corner she lurks.)[g]
13 She took hold of him[h] and kissed him
and with a brazen face she said:[i]

14 "I have fellowship offerings[l][j] at
home;
today I fulfilled my vows.
15 So I came out to meet you;
I looked for you and have found
you!
16 I have covered my bed
with colored linens from Egypt.
17 I have perfumed my bed[k]
with myrrh,[l] aloes and cinnamon.
18 Come, let's drink deep of love till
morning;
let's enjoy ourselves with love![m]
19 My husband is not at home;
he has gone on a long journey.
20 He took his purse filled with money
and will not be home till full moon."

21 With persuasive words she led him
astray;
she seduced him with her smooth
talk.[n]
22 All at once he followed her
like an ox going to the slaughter,
like a deer[m] stepping into a noose[n][o]
23 till an arrow pierces[p] his liver,
like a bird darting into a snare,
little knowing it will cost him his
life.[q]

24 Now then, my sons, listen[r] to me;
pay attention to what I say.
25 Do not let your heart turn to her ways
or stray into her paths.[s]
26 Many are the victims she has
brought down;
her slain are a mighty throng.
27 Her house is a highway to the grave,[o]
leading down to the chambers of
death.[t]

The excellency of wisdom.

8 Does not wisdom call out?[u]
Does not understanding raise her
voice?
2 On the heights along the way,
where the paths meet, she takes
her stand;
3 beside the gates leading into the city,
at the entrances, she cries aloud:[v]
4 "To you, O men, I call out;
I raise my voice to all mankind.
5 You who are simple,[w] gain
prudence;[x]
you who are foolish, gain
understanding.
6 Listen, for I have worthy things to
say;
I open my lips to speak what is
right.
7 My mouth speaks what is true,[y]
for my lips detest wickedness.
8 All the words of my mouth are just;

7:2 [a]Pr 4:4
7:3 [b]Dt 6:8; Pr 3:3
7:5 [c]ver 21; Job 31:9; Pr 2:16; 6:24
7:7 [d]Pr 1:22; 6:32
7:9 [e]Job 24:15
7:11 [f]Pr 9:13; 1Ti 5:13
7:12 [g]Pr 8:1-36; 23:26-28
7:13 [h]Ge 39:12 [i]Pr 1:20
7:14 [j]Lev 7:11-18
7:17 [k]Est 1:6; Isa 57:7; Eze 23:41; Am 6:4 [l]Ge 37:25
7:18 [m]Ge 39:7
7:21 [n]Pr 5:3
7:22 [o]Job 18:10
7:23 [p]Job 15:22; 16:13 [q]Pr 6:26; Ecc 7:26; 9:12
7:24 [r]Pr 1:8-9; 5:7; 8:32
7:25 [s]Pr 5:7-8
7:27 [t]Pr 2:18; 5:5; 9:18; Rev 22:15
8:1 [u]Pr 1:20; 9:3
8:3 [v]Job 29:7
8:5 [w]Pr 1:22 [x]Pr 1:4
8:7 [y]Ps 37:30; Jn 8:14

l*14* Traditionally *peace offerings* m*22* Syriac (see also Septuagint); Hebrew *fool* n*22* The meaning of the Hebrew for this line is uncertain. o*27* Hebrew *Sheol*

none of them is crooked or
perverse.
[9]To the discerning all of them are right;
they are faultless to those who
have knowledge.
[10]Choose my instruction instead of
silver,
knowledge rather than choice
gold,[a]
[11]for wisdom is more precious[b] than
rubies,
and nothing you desire can
compare with her.[c]

[12]"I, wisdom, dwell together with
prudence;
I possess knowledge and
discretion.[d]
[13]To fear the LORD is to hate evil;[e]
I hate[f] pride and arrogance,
evil behavior and perverse speech.
[14]Counsel and sound judgment are
mine;
I have understanding and power.[g]
[15]By me kings reign
and rulers[h] make laws that are just;
[16]by me princes govern,
and all nobles who rule on earth.[p]
[17]I love those who love me,[i]
and those who seek me find me.[j]
[18]With me are riches and honor,[k]
enduring wealth and prosperity.[l]
[19]My fruit is better than fine gold;
what I yield surpasses choice
silver.[m]
[20]I walk in the way of righteousness,
along the paths of justice,
[21]bestowing wealth on those who love
me
and making their treasuries full.[n]

[22]"The LORD brought me forth as the
first of his works,[q,r]
before his deeds of old;
[23]I was appointed[s] from eternity,
from the beginning, before the
world began.
[24]When there were no oceans, I was
given birth,
when there were no springs
abounding with water;[o]
[25]before the mountains were settled in
place,

before the hills, I was given birth,[p]
[26]before he made the earth or its fields
or any of the dust of the world.[q]
[27]I was there when he set the heavens
in place,[r]
when he marked out the horizon
on the face of the deep,
[28]when he established the clouds
above
and fixed securely the fountains of
the deep,
[29]when he gave the sea its boundary[s]
so the waters would not overstep
his command,[t]
and when he marked out the
foundations of the earth.[u]
[30] Then I was the craftsman at his
side.[v]
I was filled with delight day after day,
rejoicing always in his presence,
[31]rejoicing in his whole world
and delighting in mankind.[w]

[32]"Now then, my sons, listen to me;
blessed are[x] those who keep my
ways.[y]
[33]Listen to my instruction and be wise;
do not ignore it.
[34]Blessed is the man who listens[z] to
me,
watching daily at my doors,
waiting at my doorway.
[35]For whoever finds me[a] finds life
and receives favor from the LORD.[b]
[36]But whoever fails to find me harms
himself;[c]
all who hate me love death."

Wisdom's call.

9 Wisdom has built[d] her house;
she has hewn out its seven pillars.
[2]She has prepared her meat and
mixed her wine;
she has also set her table.[e]
[3]She has sent out her maids, and she
calls[f]
from the highest point of the city.[g]

8:10
[a]Pr 3:14-15
8:11
[b]Job 28:17-19
[c]Pr 3:13-15
8:12
[d]Pr 1:4
8:13
[e]Pr 16:6
[f]Jer 44:4
8:14
[g]Pr 21:22;
Ecc 7:19
8:15
[h]Da 2:21;
Ro 13:1
8:17
[i]1Sa 2:30;
Ps 91:14;
Jn 14:21-24
[j]Pr 1:28;
Jas 1:5
8:18
[k]Pr 3:16
[l]Dt 8:18;
Mt 6:33
8:19
[m]Pr 3:13-14;
10:20
8:21
[n]Pr 24:4
8:24
[o]Ge 7:11
8:25
[p]Job 15:7
8:26
[q]Ps 90:2
8:27
[r]Pr 3:19
8:29
[s]Ge 1:9;
Job 38:10;
Ps 16:6
[t]Ps 104:9
[u]Job 38:5
8:30
[v]Jn 1:1-3
8:31
[w]Ps 16:3;
104:1-30
8:32
[x]Lk 11:28
[y]Ps 119:1-2
8:34
[z]Pr 3:13,18
8:35
[a]Pr 3:13-18
[b]Pr 12:2
8:36
[c]Pr 15:32
9:1
[d]Eph 2:20-22;
1Pe 2:5
9:2
[e]Lk 14:16-23
9:3
[f]Pr 8:1-3
[g]ver 14

p16 Many Hebrew manuscripts and Septuagint; most
Hebrew manuscripts and nobles—all righteous rulers
q22 Or way; or dominion r22 Or The LORD
possessed me at the beginning of his work; or The
LORD brought me forth at the beginning of his work
s23 Or fashioned

4"Let all who are simple come in here!"
   she says to those who lack
      judgment.*a*
5"Come, eat my food
   and drink the wine I have mixed.*b*
6Leave your simple ways and you will
   live;*c*
   walk in the way of understanding.

7"Whoever corrects a mocker invites
   insult;
   whoever rebukes a wicked man
      incurs abuse.*d*
8Do not rebuke a mocker*e* or he will
   hate you;
   rebuke a wise man and he will
      love you.*f*
9Instruct a wise man and he will be
   wiser still;
   teach a righteous man and he will
      add to his learning.*g*

10"The fear of the LORD*h* is the
   beginning of wisdom,
   and knowledge of the Holy One is
      understanding.
11For through me your days will be
   many,
   and years will be added to your
      life.*i*
12If you are wise, your wisdom will
   reward you;
   if you are a mocker, you alone will
      suffer."

Folly's call.

13The woman Folly is loud;*j*
   she is undisciplined and without
      knowledge.*k*
14She sits at the door of her house,
   on a seat at the highest point of the
      city,*l*
15calling out to those who pass by,
   who go straight on their way.
16"Let all who are simple come in
   here!"
   she says to those who lack
      judgment.
17"Stolen water is sweet;
   food eaten in secret is delicious!*m*"
18But little do they know that the dead
   are there,

that her guests are in the depths of
   the grave.*t n*

Proverbs of Solomon: Miscellaneous.

10 The proverbs of Solomon:*o*

   A wise son brings joy to his
      father,*p*
   but a foolish son grief to his mother.

2Ill-gotten treasures are of no value,*q*
   but righteousness delivers from
      death.*r*

3The LORD does not let the righteous
   go hungry*s*
   but he thwarts the craving of the
      wicked.

4Lazy hands make a man poor,*t*
   but diligent hands bring wealth.*u*

5He who gathers crops in summer is a
   wise son,
   but he who sleeps during harvest is
      a disgraceful son.

6Blessings crown the head of the
   righteous,
   but violence overwhelms the
      mouth of the wicked.*u v*

7The memory of the righteous*w* will
   be a blessing,
   but the name of the wicked*x* will
      rot.*y*

8The wise in heart accept commands,
   but a chattering fool comes to
      ruin.*z*

9The man of integrity*a* walks
   securely,*b*
   but he who takes crooked paths
      will be found out.*c*

10He who winks maliciously*d* causes
   grief,
   and a chattering fool comes to
      ruin.

11The mouth of the righteous is a
   fountain of life,*e*
   but violence overwhelms the
      mouth of the wicked.*f*

9:4 *a*Pr 6:32
9:5 *b*Isa 55:1
9:6 *c*Pr 8:35
9:7 *d*Pr 23:9
9:8 *e*Pr 15:12
*f*Ps 141:5
9:9 *g*Pr 1:5,7
9:10 *h*Job 28:28; Pr 1:7
9:11 *i*Pr 3:16; 10:27
9:13 *j*Pr 7:11
*k*Pr 5:6
9:14 *l*ver 3
9:17 *m*Pr 20:17
9:18 *n*Pr 2:18; 7:26-27
10:1 *o*Pr 1:1
*p*Pr 15:20; 29:3
10:2 *q*Pr 21:6
*r*Pr 11:4,19
10:3 *s*Mt 6:25-34
10:4 *t*Pr 19:15
*u*Pr 12:24; 13:4; 21:5
10:6 *v*ver 8,11,14
10:7 *w*Ps 112:6
*x*Ps 109:13
*y*Ps 9:6
10:8 *z*Mt 7:24-27
10:9 *a*Isa 33:15
*b*Ps 23:4
*c*Pr 28:18
10:10 *d*Ps 35:19
10:11 *e*Ps 37:30; Pr 13:12,14,19
*f*ver 6

t18 Hebrew *Sheol*   *u6* Or *but the mouth of the wicked conceals violence*; also in verse 11

12Hatred stirs up dissension,
but love covers over all wrongs.a

13Wisdom is found on the lips of the discerning,b
but a rod is for the back of him who lacks judgment.c

14Wise men store up knowledge,
but the mouth of a fool invites ruin.d

15The wealth of the rich is their fortified city,e
but poverty is the ruin of the poor.f

16The wages of the righteous bring them life,
but the income of the wicked brings them punishment.g

17He who heeds discipline shows the way to life,h
but whoever ignores correction leads others astray.

18He who conceals his hatred has lying lips,
and whoever spreads slander is a fool.

19When words are many, sin is not absent,
but he who holds his tongue is wise.i

20The tongue of the righteous is choice silver,
but the heart of the wicked is of little value.

21The lips of the righteous nourish many,
but fools die for lack of judgment.j

22The blessing of the LORD brings wealth,k
and he adds no trouble to it.

23A fool finds pleasure in evil conduct,l
but a man of understanding delights in wisdom.

24What the wicked dreadsm will overtake him;
what the righteous desire will be granted.n

25When the storm has swept by, the wicked are gone,
but the righteous stand firmo forever.p

26As vinegar to the teeth and smoke to the eyes,
so is a sluggard to those who send him.q

27The fear of the LORD adds length to life,r
but the years of the wicked are cut short.s

28The prospect of the righteous is joy,
but the hopes of the wicked come to nothing.t

29The way of the LORD is a refuge for the righteous,
but it is the ruin of those who do evil.u

30The righteous will never be uprooted,
but the wicked will not remain in the land.v

31The mouth of the righteous brings forth wisdom,w
but a perverse tongue will be cut out.

32The lips of the righteous know what is fitting,x
but the mouth of the wicked only what is perverse.

11 The LORD abhors dishonest scales,y
but accurate weights are his delight.z

2When pride comes, then comes disgrace,a
but with humility comes wisdom.b

3The integrity of the upright guides them,
but the unfaithful are destroyed by their duplicity.c

4Wealth is worthless in the day of wrath,d
but righteousness delivers from death.e

10:12
aPr 17:9;
1Co 13:4-7;
1Pe 4:8
10:13
bver 31
cPr 26:3
10:14
dPr 18:6,7
10:15
ePr 18:11
fPr 19:7
10:16
gPr 11:18-19
10:17
hPr 6:23
10:19
iPr 17:28;
Ecc 5:3;
Jas 1:19; 3:2-12
10:21
jPr 5:22-23;
Hos 4:1,6,14
10:22
kGe 24:35;
Ps 37:22
10:23
lPr 2:14;
15:21
10:24
mIsa 66:4
nPs 145:17-19;
Mt 5:6;
1Jn 5:14-15
10:25
oPs 15:5
pPr 12:3,7;
Mt 7:24-27
10:26
qPr 26:6
10:27
rPr 9:10-11
sJob 15:32
10:28
tJob 8:13;
Pr 11:7
10:29
uPr 21:15
10:30
vPs 37:9,28-29;
Pr 2:20-22
10:31
wPs 37:30
10:32
xEcc 10:12
11:1
yLev 19:36;
Dt 25:13-16;
Pr 20:10,23
zPr 16:11
11:2
aPr 16:18
bPr 18:12;
29:23
11:3
cPr 13:6

11:4 dEze 7:19; Zep 1:18 eGe 7:1; Pr 10:2

5The righteousness of the blameless
makes a straight way for them,
but the wicked are brought down
by their own wickedness.[a]

6The righteousness of the upright
delivers them,
but the unfaithful are trapped by
evil desires.

7When a wicked man dies, his hope
perishes;
all he expected from his power
comes to nothing.[b]

8The righteous man is rescued from
trouble,
and it comes on the wicked
instead.[c]

9With his mouth the godless destroys
his neighbor,
but through knowledge the
righteous escape.

10When the righteous prosper, the city
rejoices;[d]
when the wicked perish, there are
shouts of joy.

11Through the blessing of the upright a
city is exalted,
but by the mouth of the wicked it
is destroyed.[e]

12A man who lacks judgment derides
his neighbor,[f]
but a man of understanding holds
his tongue.

13A gossip betrays a confidence,[g]
but a trustworthy man keeps a
secret.

14For lack of guidance a nation falls,[h]
but many advisers make victory
sure.[i]

15He who puts up security[j] for another
will surely suffer,
but whoever refuses to strike
hands in pledge is safe.

16A kindhearted woman gains
respect,[k]
but ruthless men gain only wealth.

17A kind man benefits himself,
but a cruel man brings trouble on
himself.

18The wicked man earns deceptive
wages,
but he who sows righteousness
reaps a sure reward.[l]

19The truly righteous man attains life,
but he who pursues evil goes to his
death.

20The LORD detests men of perverse
heart
but he delights in those whose
ways are blameless.[m]

21Be sure of this: The wicked will not
go unpunished,
but those who are righteous will go
free.[n]

22Like a gold ring in a pig's snout
is a beautiful woman who shows
no discretion.

23The desire of the righteous ends only
in good,
but the hope of the wicked only in
wrath.

24One man gives freely, yet gains even
more;
another withholds unduly, but
comes to poverty.

25A generous man will prosper;
he who refreshes others will
himself be refreshed.[o]

26People curse the man who hoards
grain,
but blessing crowns him who is
willing to sell.

27He who seeks good finds goodwill,
but evil comes to him who
searches for it.[p]

28Whoever trusts in his riches will
fall,[q]
but the righteous will thrive like a
green leaf.[r]

29He who brings trouble on his family
will inherit only wind,
and the fool will be servant to the
wise.[s]

11:5 [a]Pr 5:21-23
11:7 [b]Pr 10:28
11:8 [c]Pr 21:18
11:10 [d]Pr 28:12
11:11 [e]Pr 29:8
11:12 [f]Pr 14:21
11:13 [g]Lev 19:16; Pr 20:19; 1Ti 5:13
11:14 [h]Pr 20:18 [i]Pr 15:22; 24:6
11:15 [j]Pr 6:1
11:16 [k]Pr 31:31
11:18 [l]Hos 10:12-13
11:20 [m]1Ch 29:17; Ps 119:1; Pr 12:2,22
11:21 [n]Pr 16:5
11:25 [o]Mt 5:7; 2Co 9:6-9
11:27 [p]Est 7:10; Ps 7:15-16
11:28 [q]Job 31:24-28; Ps 49:6; 52:7; Mk 10:25; 1Ti 6:17 [r]Ps 1:3; 92:12-14; Jer 17:8
11:29 [s]Pr 14:19

³⁰The fruit of the righteous is a tree of life,ᵃ
and he who wins souls is wise.

³¹If the righteous receive their dueᵇ on earth,
how much more the ungodly and the sinner!

12 Whoever loves discipline loves knowledge,
but he who hates correction is stupid.ᶜ

²A good man obtains favor from the LORD,
but the LORD condemns a crafty man.

³A man cannot be established through wickedness,
but the righteous cannot be uprooted.ᵈ

⁴A wife of noble character is her husband's crown,
but a disgraceful wife is like decay in his bones.ᵉ

⁵The plans of the righteous are just,
but the advice of the wicked is deceitful.

⁶The words of the wicked lie in wait for blood,
but the speech of the upright rescues them.ᶠ

⁷Wicked men are overthrown and are no more,ᵍ
but the house of the righteous stands firm.ʰ

⁸A man is praised according to his wisdom,
but men with warped minds are despised.

⁹Better to be a nobody and yet have a servant
than pretend to be somebody and have no food.

¹⁰A righteous man cares for the needs of his animal,
but the kindest acts of the wicked are cruel.

¹¹He who works his land will have abundant food,
but he who chases fantasies lacks judgment.ⁱ

¹²The wicked desire the plunder of evil men,
but the root of the righteous flourishes.

¹³An evil man is trapped by his sinful talk,ʲ
but a righteous man escapes trouble.ᵏ

¹⁴From the fruit of his lips a man is filled with good thingsˡ
as surely as the work of his hands rewards him.ᵐ

¹⁵The way of a fool seems right to him,ⁿ
but a wise man listens to advice.

¹⁶A fool shows his annoyance at once,
but a prudent man overlooks an insult.ᵒ

¹⁷A truthful witness gives honest testimony,
but a false witness tells lies.ᵖ

¹⁸Reckless words pierce like a sword,q
but the tongue of the wise brings healing.ʳ

¹⁹Truthful lips endure forever,
but a lying tongue lasts only a moment.

²⁰There is deceit in the hearts of those who plot evil,
but joy for those who promote peace.

²¹No harm befalls the righteous,ˢ
but the wicked have their fill of trouble.

²²The LORD detests lying lips,ᵗ
but he delights in men who are truthful.ᵘ

²³A prudent man keeps his knowledge to himself,ᵛ
but the heart of fools blurts out folly.

11:30
ᵃJas 5:20

11:31
ᵇPr 13:21;
Jer 25:29;
1Pe 4:18

12:1
ᶜPr 9:7-9;
15:5,10,12,32

12:3
ᵈPr 10:25

12:4
ᵉPr 14:30

12:6
ᶠPr 14:3

12:7
ᵍPs 37:36
ʰPr 10:25

12:11
ⁱPr 28:19

12:13
ʲPr 18:7
ᵏPr 21:23;
2Pe 2:9

12:14
ˡPr 13:2;
15:23; 18:20
ᵐIsa 3:10-11

12:15
ⁿPr 14:12;
16:2,25;
Lk 18:11

12:16
ᵒPr 29:11

12:17
ᵖPr 14:5,25

12:18
qPs 57:4
ʳPr 15:4

12:21
ˢPs 91:10

12:22
ᵗPr 6:17;
Rev 22:15
ᵘPr 11:20

12:23
ᵛPr 10:14;
13:16

24Diligent hands will rule,
  but laziness ends in slave labor.a

25An anxious heart weighs a man down,b
  but a kind word cheers him up.

26A righteous man is cautious in
    friendship,v
  but the way of the wicked leads
    them astray.

27The lazy man does not roastw his
    game,
  but the diligent man prizes his
    possessions.

28In the way of righteousness there is
    life;c
  along that path is immortality.

13 A wise son heeds his father's
    instruction,
  but a mocker does not listen to
    rebuke.d

2From the fruit of his lips a man
    enjoys good things,e
  but the unfaithful have a craving
    for violence.

3He who guards his lipsf guards his
    life,g
  but he who speaks rashly will
    come to ruin.h

4The sluggard craves and gets nothing,
  but the desires of the diligent are
    fully satisfied.

5The righteous hate what is false,
  but the wicked bring shame and
    disgrace.

6Righteousness guards the man of
    integrity,
  but wickedness overthrows the
    sinner.i

7One man pretends to be rich, yet has
    nothing;
  another pretends to be poor, yet
    has great wealth.j

8A man's riches may ransom his life,
  but a poor man hears no threat.

9The light of the righteous shines
    brightly,

but the lamp of the wicked is
    snuffed out.k

10Pride only breeds quarrels,
  but wisdom is found in those who
    take advice.

11Dishonest money dwindles away,l
  but he who gathers money little by
    little makes it grow.

12Hope deferred makes the heart sick,
  but a longing fulfilled is a tree of
    life.

13He who scorns instruction will pay
    for it,m
  but he who respects a command is
    rewarded.

14The teaching of the wise is a
    fountain of life,n
  turning a man from the snares of
    death.o

15Good understanding wins favor,
  but the way of the unfaithful is
    hard.x

16Every prudent man acts out of
    knowledge,
  but a fool exposes his folly.p

17A wicked messenger falls into
    trouble,
  but a trustworthy envoy brings
    healing.q

18He who ignores discipline comes to
    poverty and shame,
  but whoever heeds correction is
    honored.r

19A longing fulfilled is sweet to the soul,
  but fools detest turning from evil.

20He who walks with the wise grows
    wise,
  but a companion of fools suffers
    harm.s

21Misfortune pursues the sinner,
  but prosperity is the reward of the
    righteous.t

v26 Or man is a guide to his neighbor   w27 The
meaning of the Hebrew for this word is uncertain.
x15 Or unfaithful does not endure

12:24
aPr 10:4

12:25
bPr 15:13;
Isa 50:4

12:28
cDt 30:15

13:1
dPr 10:1

13:2
ePr 12:14

13:3
fJas 3:2
gPr 21:23
hPr 18:7,20-21

13:6
iPr 11:3,5

13:7
j2Co 6:10

13:9
kJob 18:5;
Pr 4:18-19;
24:20

13:11
lPr 10:2

13:13
mNu 15:31;
2Ch 36:16

13:14
nPr 10:11
oPr 14:27

13:16
pPr 12:23

13:17
qPr 25:13

13:18
rPr 15:5,31-32

13:20
sPr 15:31

13:21
tPs 32:10

22A good man leaves an inheritance for his children's children,
but a sinner's wealth is stored up for the righteous.*a*

23A poor man's field may produce abundant food,
but injustice sweeps it away.

24He who spares the rod hates his son,
but he who loves him is careful to discipline him.*b*

25The righteous eat to their hearts' content,
but the stomach of the wicked goes hungry.*c*

14 The wise woman builds her house,*d*
but with her own hands the foolish one tears hers down.

2He whose walk is upright fears the LORD,
but he whose ways are devious despises him.

3A fool's talk brings a rod to his back,
but the lips of the wise protect them.*e*

4Where there are no oxen, the manger is empty,
but from the strength of an ox comes an abundant harvest.

5A truthful witness does not deceive,
but a false witness pours out lies.*f*

6The mocker seeks wisdom and finds none,
but knowledge comes easily to the discerning.

7Stay away from a foolish man,
for you will not find knowledge on his lips.

8The wisdom of the prudent is to give thought to their ways,
but the folly of fools is deception.*g*

9Fools mock at making amends for sin,
but goodwill is found among the upright.

10Each heart knows its own bitterness,

and no one else can share its joy.

11The house of the wicked will be destroyed,
but the tent of the upright will flourish.*h*

12There is a way that seems right to a man,*i*
but in the end it leads to death.*j*

13Even in laughter*k* the heart may ache,
and joy may end in grief.

14The faithless will be fully repaid for their ways,*l*
and the good man rewarded for his.*m*

15A simple man believes anything,
but a prudent man gives thought to his steps.

16A wise man fears the LORD and shuns evil,*n*
but a fool is hotheaded and reckless.

17A quick-tempered man does foolish things,*o*
and a crafty man is hated.

18The simple inherit folly,
but the prudent are crowned with knowledge.

19Evil men will bow down in the presence of the good,
and the wicked at the gates of the righteous.*p*

20The poor are shunned even by their neighbors,
but the rich have many friends.*q*

21He who despises his neighbor sins,*r*
but blessed is he who is kind to the needy.*s*

22Do not those who plot evil go astray?
But those who plan what is good find*y* love and faithfulness.

23All hard work brings a profit,
but mere talk leads only to poverty.

24The wealth of the wise is their crown,
but the folly of fools yields folly.

y22 Or *show*

13:22
*a*Job 27:17;
Ecc 2:26

13:24
*b*Pr 19:18;
22:15;
23:13-14;
29:15,17;
Heb 12:7

13:25
*c*Ps 34:10;
Pr 10:3

14:1
*d*Pr 24:3

14:3
*e*Pr 12:6

14:5
*f*Pr 6:19;
12:17

14:8
*g*ver 24

14:11
*h*Pr 3:33; 12:7

14:12
*i*Pr 12:15
*j*Pr 16:25

14:13
*k*Ecc 2:2

14:14
*l*Pr 1:31
*m*Pr 12:14

14:16
*n*Pr 22:3

14:17
*o*ver 29

14:19
*p*Pr 11:29

14:20
*q*Pr 19:4,7

14:21
*r*Pr 11:12
*s*Ps 41:1;
Pr 19:17

25 A truthful witness saves lives,
but a false witness is deceitful.[a]

26 He who fears the LORD has a secure fortress,[b]
and for his children it will be a refuge.

27 The fear of the LORD is a fountain of life,
turning a man from the snares of death.[c]

28 A large population is a king's glory,
but without subjects a prince is ruined.

29 A patient man has great understanding,
but a quick-tempered man displays folly.[d]

30 A heart at peace gives life to the body,
but envy rots the bones.[e]

31 He who oppresses the poor shows contempt for their Maker,[f]
but whoever is kind to the needy honors God.

32 When calamity comes, the wicked are brought down,[g]
but even in death the righteous have a refuge.[h]

33 Wisdom reposes in the heart of the discerning[i]
and even among fools she lets herself be known.[z]

34 Righteousness exalts a nation,[j]
but sin is a disgrace to any people.

35 A king delights in a wise servant,
but a shameful servant incurs his wrath.[k]

15 A gentle answer turns away wrath,[l]
but a harsh word stirs up anger.

2 The tongue of the wise commends knowledge,
but the mouth of the fool gushes folly.[m]

3 The eyes[n] of the LORD are everywhere,[o]
keeping watch on the wicked and the good.[p]

4 The tongue that brings healing is a tree of life,
but a deceitful tongue crushes the spirit.

5 A fool spurns his father's discipline,
but whoever heeds correction shows prudence.[q]

6 The house of the righteous contains great treasure,[r]
but the income of the wicked brings them trouble.

7 The lips of the wise spread knowledge;
not so the hearts of fools.

8 The LORD detests the sacrifice of the wicked,[s]
but the prayer of the upright pleases him.[t]

9 The LORD detests the way of the wicked
but he loves those who pursue righteousness.[u]

10 Stern discipline awaits him who leaves the path;
he who hates correction will die.[v]

11 Death and Destruction[a] lie open before the LORD[w]—
how much more the hearts of men![x]

12 A mocker resents correction;[y]
he will not consult the wise.

13 A happy heart makes the face cheerful,
but heartache crushes the spirit.[z]

14 The discerning heart seeks knowledge,[a]
but the mouth of a fool feeds on folly.

15 All the days of the oppressed are wretched,
but the cheerful heart has a continual feast.[b]

14:25 [a] ver 5
14:26 [b] Pr 18:10; 19:23; Isa 33:6
14:27 [c] Pr 13:14
14:29 [d] Ecc 7:8-9; Jas 1:19
14:30 [e] Pr 12:4
14:31 [f] Pr 17:5
14:32 [g] Pr 6:15 [h] Job 13:15; 2Ti 4:18
14:33 [i] Pr 2:6-10
14:34 [j] Pr 11:11
14:35 [k] Mt 24:45-51; 25:14-30
15:1 [l] Pr 25:15
15:2 [m] Pr 12:23
15:3 [n] 2Ch 16:9 [o] Job 31:4; Heb 4:13 [p] Job 34:21; Jer 16:17
15:5 [q] Pr 13:1
15:6 [r] Pr 8:21
15:8 [s] Pr 21:27; Isa 1:11; Jer 6:20 [t] ver 29
15:9 [u] Pr 21:21; 1Ti 6:11
15:10 [v] Pr 1:31-32; 5:12
15:11 [w] Job 26:6; Ps 139:8 [x] 2Ch 6:30; Ps 44:21
15:12 [y] Am 5:10
15:13 [z] Pr 12:25; 17:22; 18:14
15:14 [a] Pr 18:15
15:15 [b] ver 13

[z] *33* Hebrew; Septuagint and Syriac / *but in the heart of fools she is not known* [a] *11* Hebrew *Sheol and Abaddon*

¹⁶Better a little with the fear of the
LORD
than great wealth with turmoil.ᵃ

¹⁷Better a meal of vegetables where
there is love
than a fattened calf with hatred.ᵇ

¹⁸A hot-tempered man stirs up
dissension,ᶜ
but a patient man calms a
quarrel.ᵈ

¹⁹The way of the sluggard is blocked
with thorns,ᵉ
but the path of the upright is a
highway.

²⁰A wise son brings joy to his father,ᶠ
but a foolish man despises his
mother.

²¹Folly delights a man who lacks
judgment,ᵍ
but a man of understanding keeps
a straight course.

²²Plans fail for lack of counsel,
but with many advisers they
succeed.ʰ

²³A man finds joy in giving an apt
replyⁱ—
and how good is a timely word!ʲ

²⁴The path of life leads upward for the
wise
to keep him from going down to
the grave.ᵇ

²⁵The LORD tears down the proud
man's houseᵏ
but he keeps the widow's
boundaries intact.ˡ

²⁶The LORD detests the thoughts of the
wicked,ᵐ
but those of the pure are pleasing
to him.

²⁷A greedy man brings trouble to his
family,
but he who hates bribes will live.ⁿ

²⁸The heart of the righteous weighs its
answers,ᵒ
but the mouth of the wicked
gushes evil.

15:16
ᵃPs 37:16-17;
Pr 16:8;
1Ti 6:6

15:17
ᵇPr 17:1

15:18
ᶜPr 26:21
ᵈGe 13:8

15:19
ᵉPr 22:5

15:20
ᶠPr 10:1

15:21
ᵍPr 10:23

15:22
ʰPr 11:14

15:23
ⁱPr 12:14
ʲPr 25:11

15:25
ᵏPr 12:7
ˡDt 19:14;
Ps 68:5-6;
Pr 23:10-11

15:26
ᵐPr 6:16

15:27
ⁿEx 23:8;
Isa 33:15

15:28
ᵒ1Pe 3:15

15:29
ᵖPs 145:18-19

15:31
ᑫver 5

15:32
ʳPr 1:7

15:33
ˢPr 1:7
ᵗPr 18:12

16:1
ᵘPr 19:21

16:2
ᵛPr 21:2

16:3
ʷPs 37:5-6;
Pr 3:5-6

16:4
ˣIsa 43:7
ʸRo 9:22

16:5
ᶻPr 6:16
ᵃPr 11:20-21

16:6
ᵇPr 14:16

²⁹The LORD is far from the wicked
but he hears the prayer of the
righteous.ᵖ

³⁰A cheerful look brings joy to the
heart,
and good news gives health to the
bones.

³¹He who listens to a life-giving rebuke
will be at home among the wise.ᑫ

³²He who ignores discipline despises
himself,ʳ
but whoever heeds correction
gains understanding.

³³The fear of the LORDˢ teaches a man
wisdom,ᶜ
and humility comes before honor.ᵗ

16 To man belong the plans of the
heart,
but from the LORD comes the reply
of the tongue.ᵘ

²All a man's ways seem innocent to
him,
but motives are weighed by the
LORD.ᵛ

³Commit to the LORD whatever you do,
and your plans will succeed.ʷ

⁴The LORD works out everything for
his own endsˣ—
even the wicked for a day of
disaster.ʸ

⁵The LORD detests all the proud of
heart.ᶻ
Be sure of this: They will not go
unpunished.ᵃ

⁶Through love and faithfulness sin is
atoned for;
through the fear of the LORD a man
avoids evil.ᵇ

⁷When a man's ways are pleasing to
the LORD,
he makes even his enemies live at
peace with him.

⁸Better a little with righteousness

b24 Hebrew *Sheol*   c33 Or *Wisdom teaches the
fear of the LORD*

than much gain[a] with injustice.

[9] In his heart a man plans his course,
but the LORD determines his steps.[b]

[10] The lips of a king speak as an oracle,
and his mouth should not betray
justice.

[11] Honest scales and balances are from
the LORD;
all the weights in the bag are of his
making.[c]

[12] Kings detest wrongdoing,
for a throne is established through
righteousness.[d]

[13] Kings take pleasure in honest lips;
they value a man who speaks the
truth.[e]

[14] A king's wrath is a messenger of
death,[f]
but a wise man will appease it.

[15] When a king's face brightens, it
means life;[g]
his favor is like a rain cloud in
spring.

[16] How much better to get wisdom
than gold,
to choose understanding rather
than silver![h]

[17] The highway of the upright avoids
evil;
he who guards his way guards his
life.

[18] Pride goes before destruction,
a haughty spirit before a fall.[i]

[19] Better to be lowly in spirit and
among the oppressed
than to share plunder with the
proud.

[20] Whoever gives heed to instruction
prospers,
and blessed is he who trusts in the
LORD.[j]

[21] The wise in heart are called
discerning,
and pleasant words promote
instruction.[d][k]

[22] Understanding is a fountain of life to
those who have it,[l]
but folly brings punishment to
fools.

[23] A wise man's heart guides his
mouth,
and his lips promote instruction.[e]

[24] Pleasant words are a honeycomb,
sweet to the soul and healing to
the bones.[m]

[25] There is a way that seems right to a
man,[n]
but in the end it leads to death.[o]

[26] The laborer's appetite works for him;
his hunger drives him on.

[27] A scoundrel plots evil,
and his speech is like a scorching
fire.[p]

[28] A perverse man stirs up dissension,[q]
and a gossip separates close
friends.[r]

[29] A violent man entices his neighbor
and leads him down a path that is
not good.[s]

[30] He who winks with his eye is
plotting perversity;
he who purses his lips is bent on
evil.

[31] Gray hair is a crown of splendor;[t]
it is attained by a righteous life.

[32] Better a patient man than a warrior,
a man who controls his temper
than one who takes a city.

[33] The lot is cast into the lap,
but its every decision is from the
LORD.[u]

17

Better a dry crust with peace
and quiet
than a house full of feasting,[f] with
strife.[v]

[2] A wise servant will rule over a
disgraceful son,

16:8
[a] Ps 37:16

16:9
[b] Jer 10:23

16:11
[c] Pr 11:1

16:12
[d] Pr 25:5

16:13
[e] Pr 14:35

16:14
[f] Pr 19:12

16:15
[g] Job 29:24

16:16
[h] Pr 8:10,19

16:18
[i] Pr 11:2;
18:12

16:20
[j] Ps 2:12; 34:8;
Pr 19:8;
Jer 17:7

16:21
[k] ver 23

16:22
[l] Pr 13:14

16:24
[m] Pr 24:13-14

16:25
[n] Pr 12:15
[o] Pr 14:12

16:27
[p] Jas 3:6

16:28
[q] Pr 15:18
[r] Pr 17:9

16:29
[s] Pr 1:10;
12:26

16:31
[t] Pr 20:29

16:33
[u] Pr 18:18;
29:26

17:1
[v] Pr 15:16,17

[d] 21 Or *words make a man persuasive*   [e] 23 Or
mouth / and makes his lips persuasive   [f] 1 Hebrew
sacrifices

and will share the inheritance as one of the brothers.

3The crucible for silver and the furnace for gold,*a*
but the LORD tests the heart.*b*

4A wicked man listens to evil lips;
a liar pays attention to a malicious tongue.

5He who mocks the poor shows contempt for their Maker;*c*
whoever gloats over disaster*d* will not go unpunished.*e*

6Children's children*f* are a crown to the aged,
and parents are the pride of their children.

7Arrogant*g* lips are unsuited to a fool—
how much worse lying lips to a ruler!

8A bribe is a charm to the one who gives it;
wherever he turns, he succeeds.

9He who covers over an offense promotes love,*g*
but whoever repeats the matter separates close friends.*h*

10A rebuke impresses a man of discernment
more than a hundred lashes a fool.

11An evil man is bent only on rebellion;
a merciless official will be sent against him.

12Better to meet a bear robbed of her cubs
than a fool in his folly.

13If a man pays back evil*i* for good,
evil will never leave his house.

14Starting a quarrel is like breaching a dam;
so drop the matter before a dispute breaks out.*j*

15Acquitting the guilty and condemning the innocent*k* —

the LORD detests them both.*l*

16Of what use is money in the hand of a fool,
since he has no desire to get wisdom?*m*

17A friend loves at all times,
and a brother is born for adversity.

18A man lacking in judgment strikes hands in pledge
and puts up security for his neighbor.*n*

19He who loves a quarrel loves sin;
he who builds a high gate invites destruction.

20A man of perverse heart does not prosper;
he whose tongue is deceitful falls into trouble.

21To have a fool for a son brings grief;
there is no joy for the father of a fool.*o*

22A cheerful heart is good medicine,
but a crushed spirit dries up the bones.*p*

23A wicked man accepts a bribe*q* in secret
to pervert the course of justice.

24A discerning man keeps wisdom in view,
but a fool's eyes*r* wander to the ends of the earth.

25A foolish son brings grief to his father
and bitterness to the one who bore him.*s*

26It is not good to punish an innocent man,*t*
or to flog officials for their integrity.

27A man of knowledge uses words with restraint,
and a man of understanding is even-tempered.*u*

17:3
*a*Pr 27:21
*b*1Ch 29:17;
Ps 26:2;
Jer 17:10

17:5
*c*Pr 14:31
*d*Job 31:29
*e*Ob 1:12

17:6
*f*Pr 13:22

17:9
*g*Pr 10:12
*h*Pr 16:28

17:13
*i*Ps 109:4-5;
Jer 18:20

17:14
*j*Pr 20:3

17:15
*k*Pr 18:5
*l*Ex 23:6-7;
Isa 5:23

17:16
*m*Pr 23:23

17:18
*n*Pr 6:1-5;
11:15;
22:26-27

17:21
*o*Pr 10:1

17:22
*p*Ps 22:15;
Pr 15:13

17:23
*q*Ex 23:8

17:24
*r*Ecc 2:14

17:25
*s*Pr 10:1

17:26
*t*Pr 18:5

17:27
*u*Pr 14:29;
Jas 1:19

*g*7 Or *Eloquent*

28Even a fool is thought wise if he
    keeps silent,
and discerning if he holds his
    tongue.a

18 An unfriendly man pursues
    selfish ends;
he defies all sound judgment.

2A fool finds no pleasure in
    understanding
but delights in airing his own
    opinions.b

3When wickedness comes, so does
    contempt,
and with shame comes disgrace.

4The words of a man's mouth are
    deep waters,
but the fountain of wisdom is a
    bubbling brook.

5It is not good to be partial to the
    wickedc
or to deprive the innocent of
    justice.d

6A fool's lips bring him strife,
and his mouth invites a beating.

7A fool's mouth is his undoing,
and his lips are a snaree to his soul.f

8The words of a gossip are like choice
    morsels;
they go down to a man's inmost
    parts.g

9One who is slack in his work
is brother to one who destroys.h

10The name of the LORD is a strong
    tower;i
the righteous run to it and are safe.

11The wealth of the rich is their
    fortified city;j
they imagine it an unscalable wall.

12Before his downfall a man's heart is
    proud,
but humility comes before honor.k

13He who answers before listening—
that is his folly and his shame.l

14A man's spirit sustains him in
    sickness,

but a crushed spirit who can
    bear?m

15The heart of the discerning acquires
    knowledge;n
the ears of the wise seek it out.

16A gifto opens the way for the giver
and ushers him into the presence
    of the great.

17The first to present his case seems
    right,
till another comes forward and
    questions him.

18Casting the lot settles disputesp
and keeps strong opponents apart.

19An offended brother is more
    unyielding than a fortified city,
and disputes are like the barred
    gates of a citadel.

20From the fruit of his mouth a man's
    stomach is filled;
with the harvest from his lips he is
    satisfied.q

21The tongue has the power of life and
    death,
and those who love it will eat its
    fruit.r

22He who finds a wife finds what is
    goods
and receives favor from the LORD.t

23A poor man pleads for mercy,
but a rich man answers harshly.

24A man of many companions may
    come to ruin,
but there is a friend who sticks
    closer than a brother.u

19 Better a poor man whose walk
    is blameless
than a fool whose lips are
    perverse.v

2It is not good to have zeal without
    knowledge,
nor to be hasty and miss the way.w

3A man's own folly ruins his life,
yet his heart rages against the
    LORD.

17:28
aJob 13:5

18:2
bPr 12:23

18:5
cLev 19:15;
Pr 24:23-25;
28:21
dPs 82:2;
Pr 17:15

18:7
ePs 140:9
fPs 64:8;
Pr 10:14;
12:13; 13:3;
Ecc 10:12

18:8
gPr 26:22

18:9
hPr 28:24

18:10
i2Sa 22:3;
Ps 61:3

18:11
jPr 10:15

18:12
kPr 11:2;
15:33; 16:18

18:13
lPr 20:25;
Jn 7:51

18:14
mPr 15:13;
17:22

18:15
nPr 15:14

18:16
oGe 32:20

18:18
pPr 16:33

18:20
qPr 12:14

18:21
rPr 13:2-3;
Mt 12:37

18:22
sPr 12:4
tPr 19:14;
31:10

18:24
uPr 17:17;
Jn 15:13-15

19:1
vPr 28:6

19:2
wPr 29:20

4Wealth brings many friends,
but a poor man's friend deserts
him.*a*

5A false witness*b* will not go
unpunished,
and he who pours out lies will not
go free.*c*

6Many curry favor with a ruler,*d*
and everyone is the friend of a
man who gives gifts.*e*

7A poor man is shunned by all his
relatives—
how much more do his friends
avoid him!
Though he pursues them with
pleading,
they are nowhere to be found.*h f*

8He who gets wisdom loves his own
soul;
he who cherishes understanding
prospers.*g*

9A false witness will not go
unpunished,
and he who pours out lies will
perish.*h*

10It is not fitting for a fool*i* to live in
luxury—
how much worse for a slave to rule
over princes!*j*

11A man's wisdom gives him
patience;*k*
it is to his glory to overlook an
offense.

12A king's rage is like the roar of a
lion,
but his favor is like dew*l* on the
grass.*m*

13A foolish son is his father's ruin,*n*
and a quarrelsome wife is like a
constant dripping.*o*

14Houses and wealth are inherited
from parents,*p*
but a prudent wife is from the
LORD.*q*

15Laziness brings on deep sleep,
and the shiftless man goes hungry.*r*

16He who obeys instructions guards
his life,
but he who is contemptuous of his
ways will die.*s*

17He who is kind to the poor lends to
the LORD,
and he will reward him for what
he has done.*t*

18Discipline your son, for in that there
is hope;
do not be a willing party to his
death.*u*

19A hot-tempered man must pay the
penalty;
if you rescue him, you will have to
do it again.

20Listen to advice and accept
instruction,*v*
and in the end you will be wise.*w*

21Many are the plans in a man's heart,
but it is the LORD's purpose that
prevails.*x*

22What a man desires is unfailing love *i*;
better to be poor than a liar.

23The fear of the LORD leads to life:
Then one rests content, untouched
by trouble.*y*

24The sluggard buries his hand in the
dish;
he will not even bring it back to
his mouth!*z*

25Flog a mocker, and the simple will
learn prudence;
rebuke a discerning man, and he
will gain knowledge.*a*

26He who robs his father and drives
out his mother*b*
is a son who brings shame and
disgrace.

27Stop listening to instruction, my son,
and you will stray from the words
of knowledge.

28A corrupt witness mocks at justice,

19:4
a Pr 14:20

19:5
b Ex 23:1
c Dt 19:19;
Pr 21:28

19:6
d Pr 29:26
e Pr 17:8;
18:16

19:7
f ver 4;
Ps 38:11

19:8
g Pr 16:20

19:9
h ver 5

19:10
i Pr 26:1
j Pr 30:21-23;
Ecc 10:5-7

19:11
k Pr 16:32

19:12
l Ps 133:3
m Pr 16:14-15

19:13
n Pr 10:1
o Pr 21:9

19:14
p 2Co 12:14
q Pr 18:22

19:15
r Pr 6:9; 10:4

19:16
s Pr 16:17;
Lk 10:28

19:17
t Mt 10:42;
2Co 9:6-8

19:18
u Pr 13:24;
23:13-14

19:20
v Pr 4:1
w Pr 12:15

19:21
x Ps 33:11;
Pr 16:9;
Isa 14:24,27

19:23
y Ps 25:13;
Pr 12:21;
1Ti 4:8

19:24
z Pr 26:15

19:25
a Pr 9:9; 21:11

19:26
b Pr 28:24

h 7 The meaning of the Hebrew for this sentence is
uncertain.   i 22 Or *A man's greed is his shame*

and the mouth of the wicked gulps
down evil.*a*

29Penalties are prepared for mockers,
and beatings for the backs of
fools.*b*

20 Wine is a mocker and beer a
brawler;
whoever is led astray by them is
not wise.*c*

2A king's wrath is like the roar of a
lion;*d*
he who angers him forfeits his
life.*e*

3It is to a man's honor to avoid strife,
but every fool is quick to quarrel.*f*

4A sluggard does not plow in season;
so at harvest time he looks but
finds nothing.

5The purposes of a man's heart are
deep waters,
but a man of understanding draws
them out.

6Many a man claims to have unfailing
love,
but a faithful man who can find?*g*

7The righteous man leads a blameless
life;
blessed are his children after him.*h*

8When a king sits on his throne to
judge,
he winnows out all evil with his
eyes.*i*

9Who can say, "I have kept my heart
pure;
I am clean and without sin"?*j*

10Differing weights and differing
measures—
the LORD detests them both.*k*

11Even a child is known by his actions,
by whether his conduct is pure*l*
and right.

12Ears that hear and eyes that see—
the LORD has made them both.*m*

13Do not love sleep or you will grow
poor;*n*

stay awake and you will have food
to spare.

14"It's no good, it's no good!" says the
buyer;
then off he goes and boasts about
his purchase.

15Gold there is, and rubies in
abundance,
but lips that speak knowledge are a
rare jewel.

16Take the garment of one who puts
up security for a stranger;
hold it in pledge*o* if he does it for a
wayward woman.*p*

17Food gained by fraud tastes sweet to
a man,*q*
but he ends up with a mouth full of
gravel.

18Make plans by seeking advice;
if you wage war, obtain guidance.*r*

19A gossip betrays a confidence;*s*
so avoid a man who talks too much.

20If a man curses his father or mother,*t*
his lamp will be snuffed out in
pitch darkness.*u*

21An inheritance quickly gained at the
beginning
will not be blessed at the end.

22Do not say, "I'll pay you back for this
wrong!"*v*
Wait for the LORD, and he will
deliver you.*w*

23The LORD detests differing weights,
and dishonest scales do not please
him.*x*

24A man's steps are directed by the
LORD.
How then can anyone understand
his own way?*y*

25It is a trap for a man to dedicate
something rashly
and only later to consider his
vows.*z*

26A wise king winnows out the
wicked;

19:28
*a*Job 15:16

19:29
*b*Pr 26:3

20:1
*c*Pr 31:4

20:2
*d*Pr 19:12
*e*Pr 8:36

20:3
*f*Pr 17:14

20:6
*g*Ps 12:1

20:7
*h*Ps 37:25-26;
112:2

20:8
*i*ver 26;
Pr 25:4-5

20:9
*j*1Ki 8:46;
Ecc 7:20;
1Jn 1:8

20:10
*k*ver 23;
Pr 11:1

20:11
*l*Mt 7:16

20:12
*m*Ps 94:9

20:13
*n*Pr 6:11;
19:15

20:16
*o*Ex 22:26
*p*Pr 27:13

20:17
*q*Pr 9:17

20:18
*r*Pr 11:14;
24:6

20:19
*s*Pr 11:13

20:20
*t*Pr 30:11
*u*Ex 21:17;
Job 18:5

20:22
*v*Pr 24:29
*w*Ro 12:19

20:23
*x*ver 10

20:24
*y*Jer 10:23

20:25
*z*Ecc 5:2,4-5

he drives the threshing wheel over them.*a*

27The lamp of the LORD searches the spirit of a man j;
it searches out his inmost being.

28Love and faithfulness keep a king safe;
through love his throne is made secure.*b*

29The glory of young men is their strength,
gray hair the splendor of the old.*c*

30Blows and wounds cleanse*d* away evil,
and beatings purge the inmost being.

21 The king's heart is in the hand of the LORD;
he directs it like a watercourse wherever he pleases.

2All a man's ways seem right to him,
but the LORD weighs the heart.*e*

3To do what is right and just
is more acceptable to the LORD than sacrifice.*f*

4Haughty eyes *g* and a proud heart,
the lamp of the wicked, are sin!

5The plans of the diligent lead to profit*h*
as surely as haste leads to poverty.

6A fortune made by a lying tongue
is a fleeting vapor and a deadly snare.*k i*

7The violence of the wicked will drag them away,
for they refuse to do what is right.

8The way of the guilty is devious,*j*
but the conduct of the innocent is upright.

9Better to live on a corner of the roof
than share a house with a quarrelsome wife.*k*

10The wicked man craves evil;
his neighbor gets no mercy from him.

11When a mocker is punished, the simple gain wisdom;
when a wise man is instructed, he gets knowledge.*l*

12The Righteous Onel takes note of the house of the wicked
and brings the wicked to ruin.*m*

13If a man shuts his ears to the cry of the poor,
he too will cry out and not be answered.*n*

14A gift given in secret soothes anger,
and a bribe concealed in the cloak pacifies great wrath.*o*

15When justice is done, it brings joy to the righteous
but terror to evildoers.*p*

16A man who strays from the path of understanding
comes to rest in the company of the dead.*q*

17He who loves pleasure will become poor;
whoever loves wine and oil will never be rich.*r*

18The wicked become a ransom*s* for the righteous,
and the unfaithful for the upright.

19Better to live in a desert
than with a quarrelsome and ill-tempered wife.*t*

20In the house of the wise are stores of choice food and oil,
but a foolish man devours all he has.

21He who pursues righteousness and love
finds life, prosperity*m* and honor.*u*

22A wise man attacks the city of the mighty*v*
and pulls down the stronghold in which they trust.

Cross references (center column):

20:26 *a*ver 8
20:28 *b*Pr 29:14
20:29 *c*Pr 16:31
20:30 *d*Pr 22:15
21:2 *e*Pr 16:2; 24:12; Lk 16:15
21:3 *f*1Sa 15:22; Pr 15:8; Isa 1:11; Hos 6:6; Mic 6:6-8
21:4 *g*Pr 6:17
21:5 *h*Pr 10:4; 28:22
21:6 *i*2Pe 2:3
21:8 *j*Pr 2:15
21:9 *k*Pr 25:24
21:11 *l*Pr 19:25
21:12 *m*Pr 14:11
21:13 *n*Mt 18:30-34; Jas 2:13
21:14 *o*Pr 18:16; 19:6
21:15 *p*Pr 10:29
21:16 *q*Ps 49:14
21:17 *r*Pr 23:20-21, 29-35
21:18 *s*Pr 11:8; Isa 43:3
21:19 *t*ver 9
21:21 *u*Mt 5:6
21:22 *v*Ecc 9:15-16

j27 Or *The spirit of man is the LORD's lamp*
k6 Some Hebrew manuscripts, Septuagint and Vulgate; most Hebrew manuscripts *vapor for those who seek death*   l12 Or *The righteous man*   m21 Or *righteousness*

²³He who guards his mouth*a* and his
tongue
keeps himself from calamity.*b*

²⁴The proud and arrogant*c*
man—"Mocker" is his name;
he behaves with overweening pride.

²⁵The sluggard's craving will be the
death of him,*d*
because his hands refuse to work.

²⁶All day long he craves for more,
but the righteous give without
sparing.*e*

²⁷The sacrifice of the wicked is
detestable*f*—
how much more so when brought
with evil intent!*g*

²⁸A false witness will perish,*h*
and whoever listens to him will be
destroyed forever.*ⁿ*

²⁹A wicked man puts up a bold front,
but an upright man gives thought
to his ways.

³⁰There is no wisdom,*i* no insight, no
plan
that can succeed against the LORD.*j*

³¹The horse is made ready for the day
of battle,
but victory rests with the LORD.*k*

22 A good name is more desirable
than great riches;
to be esteemed is better than silver
or gold.*l*

²Rich and poor have this in common:
The LORD is the Maker of them all.*m*

³A prudent man sees danger and
takes refuge,*n*
but the simple keep going and
suffer for it.*o*

⁴Humility and the fear of the LORD
bring wealth and honor and life.

⁵In the paths of the wicked lie thorns
and snares,*p*
but he who guards his soul stays
far from them.

⁶Train*o* a child in the way he should go,*q*

21:23
*a*Jas 3:2
*b*Pr 12:13;
13:3

21:24
*c*Ps 1:1;
Pr 1:22;
Isa 16:6;
Jer 48:29

21:25
*d*Pr 13:4

21:26
*e*Ps 37:26;
Mt 5:42;
Eph 4:28

21:27
*f*Isa 66:3;
Jer 6:20;
Am 5:2
*g*Pr 15:8

21:28
*h*Pr 19:5

21:30
*i*Jer 9:23
*j*Isa 8:10;
Ac 5:39

21:31
*k*Ps 3:8;
33:12-19;
Isa 31:1

22:1
*l*Ecc 7:1

22:2
*m*Job 31:15

22:3
*n*Pr 14:16
*o*Pr 27:12

22:5
*p*Pr 15:19

22:6
*q*Eph 6:4

22:8
*r*Job 4:8
*s*Ps 125:3

22:9
*t*2Co 9:6
*u*Pr 19:17

22:10
*v*Pr 18:6;
26:20

22:11
*w*Pr 16:13;
Mt 5:8

22:13
*x*Pr 26:13

22:14
*y*Pr 2:16;
5:3-5; 7:5;
23:27
*z*Ecc 7:26

22:15
*a*Pr 13:24;
23:14

22:17
*b*Pr 5:1

and when he is old he will not turn
from it.

⁷The rich rule over the poor,
and the borrower is servant to the
lender.

⁸He who sows wickedness reaps
trouble,*r*
and the rod of his fury will be
destroyed.*s*

⁹A generous man will himself be
blessed,*t*
for he shares his food with the
poor.*u*

¹⁰Drive out the mocker, and out goes
strife;
quarrels and insults are ended.*v*

¹¹He who loves a pure heart and
whose speech is gracious
will have the king for his friend.*w*

¹²The eyes of the LORD keep watch
over knowledge,
but he frustrates the words of the
unfaithful.

¹³The sluggard says, "There is a lion
outside!"*x*
or, "I will be murdered in the
streets!"

¹⁴The mouth of an adulteress is a deep
pit;*y*
he who is under the LORD's wrath
will fall into it.*z*

¹⁵Folly is bound up in the heart of a
child,
but the rod of discipline will drive
it far from him.*a*

¹⁶He who oppresses the poor to
increase his wealth
and he who gives gifts to the
rich—both come to poverty.

Sayings of the wise.

¹⁷Pay attention and listen to the
sayings of the wise;*b*
apply your heart to what I teach,

ⁿ28 Or / but the words of an obedient man will live
on   *o6* Or Start

320

¹⁸for it is pleasing when you keep
them in your heart
and have all of them ready on your
lips.
¹⁹So that your trust may be in the LORD,
I teach you today, even you.
²⁰Have I not written thirty ᵖ sayings for
you,
sayings of counsel and knowledge,
²¹teaching you true and reliable
words,ᵃ
so that you can give sound answers
to him who sent you?

²²Do not exploit the poorᵇ because
they are poor
and do not crush the needy in
court,ᶜ
²³for the LORD will take up their case ᵈ
and will plunder those who
plunder them.ᵉ

²⁴Do not make friends with a hot-
tempered man,
do not associate with one easily
angered,
²⁵or you may learn his ways
and get yourself ensnared. ᶠ

²⁶Do not be a man who strikes hands
in pledgeᵍ
or puts up security for debts;
²⁷if you lack the means to pay,
your very bed will be snatched
from under you.ʰ

²⁸Do not move an ancient boundary
stoneⁱ
set up by your forefathers.

²⁹Do you see a man skilled in his
work?
He will serveʲ before kings;
he will not serve before obscure
men.

23 When you sit to dine with a
ruler,
note well whatᑫ is before you,
²and put a knife to your throat
if you are given to gluttony.
³Do not crave his delicacies, ᵏ
for that food is deceptive.

⁴Do not wear yourself out to get rich;

have the wisdom to show restraint.
⁵Cast but a glance at riches, and they
are gone,
for they will surely sprout wings
and fly off to the sky like an eagle. ˡ

⁶Do not eat the food of a stingy man,
do not crave his delicacies; ᵐ
⁷for he is the kind of man
who is always thinking about the
cost.ʳ
"Eat and drink," he says to you,
but his heart is not with you.
⁸You will vomit up the little you have
eaten
and will have wasted your
compliments.

⁹Do not speak to a fool,
for he will scorn the wisdom of
your words.ⁿ

¹⁰Do not move an ancient boundary
stoneᵒ
or encroach on the fields of the
fatherless,
¹¹for their Defenderᵖ is strong;
he will take up their case against
you.ᑫ

¹²Apply your heart to instruction
and your ears to words of
knowledge.

¹³Do not withhold discipline from a
child;
if you punish him with the rod, he
will not die.
¹⁴Punish him with the rod
and save his soul from death.ˢ

¹⁵My son, if your heart is wise,
then my heart will be glad;
¹⁶my inmost being will rejoice
when your lips speak what is
right.ʳ

¹⁷Do not let your heart envyˢ sinners,
but always be zealous for the fear
of the LORD.
¹⁸There is surely a future hope for you,

22:21 ᵃLk 1:3-4; 1Pe 3:15
22:22 ᵇZec 7:10 ᶜEx 23:6; Mal 3:5
22:23 ᵈPs 12:5 ᵉ1Sa 25:39; Pr 23:10-11
22:25 ᶠ1Co 15:33
22:26 ᵍPr 11:15
22:27 ʰPr 17:18
22:28 ⁱDt 19:14; Pr 23:10
22:29 ʲGe 41:46
23:3 ᵏver 6-8
23:5 ˡPr 27:24
23:6 ᵐPs 141:4
23:9 ⁿPr 1:7; 9:7; Mt 7:6
23:10 ᵒDt 19:14; Pr 22:28
23:11 ᵖJob 19:25 ᑫPr 22:22-23
23:16 ʳver 24; Pr 27:11
23:17 ˢPs 37:1; Pr 28:14

ᵖ20 Or *not formerly written*; or *not written excellent* ᑫ1 Or *who* ʳ7 Or *for as he thinks within himself, / so he is*; or *for as he puts on a feast, / so he is* ˢ14 Hebrew *Sheol*

321

and your hope will not be cut off.*a*

¹⁹Listen, my son, and be wise,
and keep your heart on the right
path.
²⁰Do not join those who drink too
much wine*b*
or gorge themselves on meat,
²¹for drunkards and gluttons become
poor,*c*
and drowsiness clothes them in
rags.

²²Listen to your father, who gave you
life,
and do not despise your mother
when she is old.*d*
²³Buy the truth and do not sell it;
get wisdom, discipline and
understanding.*e*
²⁴The father of a righteous man has
great joy;
he who has a wise son delights in
him.*f*
²⁵May your father and mother be glad;
may she who gave you birth
rejoice!

²⁶My son,*g* give me your heart
and let your eyes keep to my
ways,*h*
²⁷for a prostitute is a deep pit*i*
and a wayward wife is a narrow
well.
²⁸Like a bandit she lies in wait,*j*
and multiplies the unfaithful
among men.

²⁹Who has woe? Who has sorrow?
Who has strife? Who has
complaints?
Who has needless bruises? Who
has bloodshot eyes?
³⁰Those who linger over wine,*k*
who go to sample bowls of mixed
wine.
³¹Do not gaze at wine when it is red,
when it sparkles in the cup,
when it goes down smoothly!
³²In the end it bites like a snake
and poisons like a viper.
³³Your eyes will see strange sights
and your mind imagine confusing
things.

23:18
a Ps 9:18;
Pr 24:14,19-20

23:20
b Isa 5:11,22;
Ro 13:13;
Eph 5:18

23:21
c Pr 21:17

23:22
d Lev 19:32;
Pr 1:8; 30:17;
Eph 6:1-2

23:23
e Pr 4:7

23:24
f ver 15-16;
Pr 10:1;
15:20

23:26
g Pr 3:1; 5:1-6
h Ps 18:21;
Pr 4:4

23:27
i Pr 22:14

23:28
j Pr 7:11-12;
Ecc 7:26

23:30
k Ps 75:8;
Isa 5:11;
Eph 5:18

24:1
l Ps 37:1;
73:3;
Pr 3:31-32;
23:17-18

24:2
m Ps 10:7

24:3
n Pr 14:1

24:4
o Pr 8:21

24:6
p Pr 11:14;
20:18;
Lk 14:31

24:10
q Job 4:5;
Jer 51:46;
Heb 12:3

24:11
r Ps 82:4;
Isa 58:6-7

24:12
s Pr 21:2
t Job 34:11;
Ps 62:12;
Ro 2:6*

³⁴You will be like one sleeping on the
high seas,
lying on top of the rigging.
³⁵"They hit me," you will say, "but I'm
not hurt!
They beat me, but I don't feel it!
When will I wake up
so I can find another drink?"

24 Do not envy*l* wicked men,
do not desire their company;
²for their hearts plot violence,
and their lips talk about making
trouble.*m*

³By wisdom a house is built,*n*
and through understanding it is
established;
⁴through knowledge its rooms are filled
with rare and beautiful treasures.*o*

⁵A wise man has great power,
and a man of knowledge increases
strength;
⁶for waging war you need guidance,
and for victory many advisers.*p*

⁷Wisdom is too high for a fool;
in the assembly at the gate he has
nothing to say.

⁸He who plots evil
will be known as a schemer.
⁹The schemes of folly are sin,
and men detest a mocker.

¹⁰If you falter in times of trouble,
how small is your strength!*q*

¹¹Rescue those being led away to
death;
hold back those staggering toward
slaughter.*r*
¹²If you say, "But we knew nothing
about this,"
does not he who weighs*s* the heart
perceive it?
Does not he who guards your life
know it?
Will he not repay each person
according to what he has
done?*t*

¹³Eat honey, my son, for it is good;
honey from the comb is sweet to
your taste.

[14]Know also that wisdom is sweet to
your soul;
if you find it, there is a future hope
for you,
and your hope will not be cut off.[a b]

[15]Do not lie in wait like an outlaw
against a righteous man's house,
do not raid his dwelling place;
[16]for though a righteous man falls
seven times, he rises again,
but the wicked are brought down
by calamity. [c]

[17]Do not gloat[d] when your enemy
falls;
when he stumbles, do not let your
heart rejoice,[e]
[18]or the LORD will see and disapprove
and turn his wrath away from him.

[19]Do not fret[f] because of evil men
or be envious of the wicked,
[20]for the evil man has no future hope,
and the lamp of the wicked will be
snuffed out.[g]

[21]Fear the LORD and the king,[h] my son,
and do not join with the
rebellious,
[22]for those two will send sudden
destruction upon them,
and who knows what calamities
they can bring?

More sayings of the wise.

[23]These also are sayings of the wise:[i]

To show partiality[j] in judging is not
good:[k]
[24]Whoever says to the guilty, "You are
innocent"[l]—
peoples will curse him and nations
denounce him.
[25]But it will go well with those who
convict the guilty,
and rich blessing will come upon
them.

[26]An honest answer
is like a kiss on the lips.

[27]Finish your outdoor work
and get your fields ready;
after that, build your house.

24:14
[a]Ps 119:103;
Pr 16:24
[b]Pr 23:18

24:16
[c]Job 5:19;
Ps 34:19;
Mic 7:8

24:17
[d]Ob 1:12
[e]Job 31:29

24:19
[f]Ps 37:1

24:20
[g]Job 18:5;
Pr 13:9;
23:17-18

24:21
[h]Ro 13:1-5;
1Pe 2:17

24:23
[i]Pr 1:6
[j]Lev 19:15
[k]Pr 28:21

24:24
[l]Pr 17:15

24:28
[m]Ps 7:4;
Pr 25:18;
Eph 4:25

24:29
[n]Pr 20:22;
Mt 5:38-41;
Ro 12:17

24:30
[o]Pr 6:6-11;
26:13-16

24:33
[p]Pr 6:10

24:34
[q]Pr 10:4;
Ecc 10:18

25:1
[r]1Ki 4:32
[s]Pr 1:1

25:2
[t]Pr 16:10-15

25:5
[u]Pr 20:8
[v]2Sa 7:13
[w]Pr 16:12;
29:14

[28]Do not testify against your neighbor
without cause,[m]
or use your lips to deceive.
[29]Do not say, "I'll do to him as he has
done to me;
I'll pay that man back for what he
did."[n]

[30]I went past the field of the
sluggard,[o]
past the vineyard of the man who
lacks judgment;
[31]thorns had come up everywhere,
the ground was covered with weeds,
and the stone wall was in ruins.
[32]I applied my heart to what I
observed
and learned a lesson from what I
saw:
[33]A little sleep, a little slumber,
a little folding of the hands to
rest[p]—
[34]and poverty will come on you like a
bandit
and scarcity like an armed man.[t q]

Proverbs of Solomon: Kings.

25 These are more proverbs[r] of Solomon, copied by the men of Hez-
ekiah king of Judah:[s]

[2]It is the glory of God to conceal a
matter;
to search out a matter is the glory
of kings.[t]

[3]As the heavens are high and the
earth is deep,
so the hearts of kings are
unsearchable.

[4]Remove the dross from the silver,
and out comes material for[u] the
silversmith;
[5]remove the wicked from the king's
presence,[u]
and his throne will be established[v]
through righteousness.[w]

[6]Do not exalt yourself in the king's
presence,

[t]34 Or like a vagrant / and scarcity like a beggar
[u]4 Or comes a vessel from

and do not claim a place among
  great men;
7it is better for him to say to you,
  "Come up here,"*a*
than for him to humiliate you
  before a nobleman.

Neighbors.

What you have seen with your eyes
8 do not bring *v* hastily to court,
for what will you do in the end
  if your neighbor puts you to shame? *b*

9If you argue your case with a neighbor,
  do not betray another man's
    confidence,
10or he who hears it may shame you
  and you will never lose your bad
    reputation.

11A word aptly spoken
  is like apples of gold in settings of
    silver.*c*

12Like an earring of gold or an
    ornament of fine gold
  is a wise man's rebuke to a
    listening ear.*d*

13Like the coolness of snow at harvest
    time
  is a trustworthy messenger to
    those who send him;
  he refreshes the spirit of his
    masters.*e*

14Like clouds and wind without rain
  is a man who boasts of gifts he
    does not give.

15Through patience a ruler can be
    persuaded,*f*
  and a gentle tongue can break a
    bone.*g*

16If you find honey, eat just enough—
  too much of it, and you will vomit.*h*
17Seldom set foot in your neighbor's
    house—
  too much of you, and he will hate you.

18Like a club or a sword or a sharp arrow
  is the man who gives false
    testimony against his
    neighbor. *i*

19Like a bad tooth or a lame foot
  is reliance on the unfaithful in
    times of trouble.

20Like one who takes away a garment
    on a cold day,
  or like vinegar poured on soda,
  is one who sings songs to a heavy
    heart.

Enemies.

21If your enemy is hungry, give him
    food to eat;
  if he is thirsty, give him water to
    drink.
22In doing this, you will heap burning
    coals *j* on his head,
  and the LORD will reward you. *k*

23As a north wind brings rain,
  so a sly tongue brings angry looks.

24Better to live on a corner of the roof
  than share a house with a
    quarrelsome wife. *l*

25Like cold water to a weary soul
  is good news from a distant land. *m*

26Like a muddied spring or a polluted
    well
  is a righteous man who gives way
    to the wicked.

27It is not good to eat too much honey, *n*
  nor is it honorable to seek one's
    own honor. *o*

28Like a city whose walls are broken
    down
  is a man who lacks self-control.

Fools.

26 Like snow in summer or rain *p*
    in harvest,
  honor is not fitting for a fool. *q*

2Like a fluttering sparrow or a darting
    swallow,
  an undeserved curse does not
    come to rest. *r*

25:7
*a*Lk 14:7-10

25:8
*b*Mt 5:25-26

25:11
*c*ver 12;
Pr 15:23

25:12
*d*ver 11;
Ps 141:5;
Pr 13:18;
15:31

25:13
*e*Pr 10:26;
13:17

25:15
*f*Ecc 10:4
*g*Pr 15:1

25:16
*h*ver 27

25:18
*i*Ps 57:4;
Pr 12:18

25:22
*j*Ps 18:8
*k*2Sa 16:12;
2Ch 28:15;
Mt 5:44;
Ro 12:20*

25:24
*l*Pr 21:9

25:25
*m*Pr 15:30

25:27
*n*ver 16
*o*Pr 27:2;
Mt 23:12

26:1
*p*1Sa 12:17
*q*ver 8;
Pr 19:10

26:2
*r*Nu 23:8;
Dt 23:5

*v*7,8 Or *nobleman / on whom you had set your
eyes. / 8Do not go*

³A whip for the horse, a halter for the donkey,[a]
and a rod for the backs of fools![b]

⁴Do not answer a fool according to his folly,
or you will be like him yourself.[c]

⁵Answer a fool according to his folly,
or he will be wise in his own eyes.[d]

⁶Like cutting off one's feet or drinking violence
is the sending of a message by the hand of a fool.[e]

⁷Like a lame man's legs that hang limp
is a proverb in the mouth of a fool.[f]

⁸Like tying a stone in a sling
is the giving of honor to a fool.[g]

⁹Like a thornbush in a drunkard's hand
is a proverb in the mouth of a fool.[h]

¹⁰Like an archer who wounds at random
is he who hires a fool or any passer-by.

¹¹As a dog returns to its vomit,[i]
so a fool repeats his folly.[j]

¹²Do you see a man wise in his own eyes?[k]
There is more hope for a fool than for him.[l]

The sluggard.

¹³The sluggard says,[m] "There is a lion in the road,
a fierce lion roaming the streets!"[n]

¹⁴As a door turns on its hinges,
so a sluggard turns on his bed.[o]

¹⁵The sluggard buries his hand in the dish;
he is too lazy to bring it back to his mouth.[p]

¹⁶The sluggard is wiser in his own eyes
than seven men who answer discreetly.

Speech.

¹⁷Like one who seizes a dog by the ears
is a passer-by who meddles in a quarrel not his own.

¹⁸Like a madman shooting firebrands or deadly arrows
¹⁹is a man who deceives his neighbor
and says, "I was only joking!"

²⁰Without wood a fire goes out;
without gossip a quarrel dies down.[q]

²¹As charcoal to embers and as wood to fire,
so is a quarrelsome man for kindling strife.[r]

²²The words of a gossip are like choice morsels;
they go down to a man's inmost parts.[s]

²³Like a coating of glaze[w] over earthenware
are fervent lips with an evil heart.

²⁴A malicious man disguises himself with his lips,[t]
but in his heart he harbors deceit.[u]

²⁵Though his speech is charming,[v] do not believe him,
for seven abominations fill his heart.[w]

²⁶His malice may be concealed by deception,
but his wickedness will be exposed in the assembly.

²⁷If a man digs a pit,[x] he will fall into it;[y]
if a man rolls a stone, it will roll back on him.[z]

²⁸A lying tongue hates those it hurts,
and a flattering mouth[a] works ruin.

Miscellaneous proverbs.

27 Do not boast[b] about tomorrow,
for you do not know what a day may bring forth.[c]

Cross references (center column)

26:3
[a]Ps 32:9
[b]Pr 10:13

26:4
[c]ver 5;
Isa 36:21

26:5
[d]ver 4; Pr 3:7

26:6
[e]Pr 10:26

26:7
[f]ver 9

26:8
[g]ver 1

26:9
[h]ver 7

26:11
[i]2Pe 2:22*
[j]Ex 8:15;
Ps 85:8

26:12
[k]Pr 3:7
[l]Pr 29:20

26:13
[m]Pr 6:6-11;
24:30-34
[n]Pr 22:13

26:14
[o]Pr 6:9

26:15
[p]Pr 19:24

26:20
[q]Pr 22:10

26:21
[r]Pr 14:17;
15:18

26:22
[s]Pr 18:8

26:24
[t]Ps 31:18
[u]Ps 41:6;
Pr 10:18;
12:20

26:25
[v]Ps 28:3
[w]Jer 9:4-8

26:27
[x]Ps 7:15
[y]Est 6:13
[z]Est 2:23;
7:9; Ps 35:8;
141:10;
Pr 28:10;
29:6;
Isa 50:11

26:28
[a]Ps 12:3;
Pr 29:5

27:1
[b]1Ki 20:11
[c]Mt 6:34;
Lk 12:19-20;
Jas 4:13-16

w23 With a different word division of the Hebrew; Masoretic Text *of silver dross*

2Let another praise you, and not your
own mouth;
someone else, and not your own
lips.[a]

3Stone is heavy and sand[b] a burden,
but provocation by a fool is heavier
than both.

4Anger is cruel and fury
overwhelming,
but who can stand before jealousy?[c]

5Better is open rebuke
than hidden love.

6Wounds from a friend can be trusted,
but an enemy multiplies kisses.[d]

7He who is full loathes honey,
but to the hungry even what is
bitter tastes sweet.

8Like a bird that strays from its nest[e]
is a man who strays from his
home.

9Perfume[f] and incense bring joy to
the heart,
and the pleasantness of one's
friend springs from his earnest
counsel.

10Do not forsake your friend and the
friend of your father,
and do not go to your brother's
house when disaster[g] strikes
you—
better a neighbor nearby than a
brother far away.

11Be wise, my son, and bring joy to my
heart;[h]
then I can answer anyone who
treats me with contempt.[i]

12The prudent see danger and take
refuge,
but the simple keep going and
suffer for it.[j]

13Take the garment of one who puts
up security for a stranger;
hold it in pledge if he does it for a
wayward woman.[k]

14If a man loudly blesses his neighbor
early in the morning,
it will be taken as a curse.

15A quarrelsome wife is like
a constant dripping[l] on a rainy day;
16restraining her is like restraining the
wind
or grasping oil with the hand.

17As iron sharpens iron,
so one man sharpens another.

18He who tends a fig tree will eat its
fruit,[m]
and he who looks after his master
will be honored.[n]

19As water reflects a face,
so a man's heart reflects the man.

20Death and Destruction[x] are never
satisfied,[o]
and neither are the eyes of man.[p]

21The crucible for silver and the
furnace for gold,[q]
but man is tested by the praise he
receives.

22Though you grind a fool in a mortar,
grinding him like grain with a
pestle,
you will not remove his folly from
him.

23Be sure you know the condition of
your flocks,[r]
give careful attention to your
herds;
24for riches do not endure forever,[s]
and a crown is not secure for all
generations.
25When the hay is removed and new
growth appears
and the grass from the hills is
gathered in,
26the lambs will provide you with
clothing,
and the goats with the price of a
field.
27You will have plenty of goats' milk
to feed you and your family
and to nourish your servant girls.

27:2 [a]Pr 25:27
27:3 [b]Job 6:3
27:4 [c]Nu 5:14
27:6 [d]Ps 141:5; Pr 28:23
27:8 [e]Isa 16:2
27:9 [f]Est 2:12; Ps 45:8
27:10 [g]Pr 17:17; 18:24
27:11 [h]Pr 10:1; 23:15-16 [i]Ge 24:60
27:12 [j]Pr 22:3
27:13 [k]Pr 20:16
27:15 [l]Est 1:18; Pr 19:13
27:18 [m]1Co 9:7 [n]Lk 19:12-27
27:20 [o]Pr 30:15-16; Hab 2:5 [p]Ecc 1:8; 6:7
27:21 [q]Pr 17:3
27:23 [r]Pr 12:10
27:24 [s]Pr 23:5

[x]20 Hebrew *Sheol and Abaddon*

28

The wicked man flees[a] though no one pursues,[b]
but the righteous are as bold as a lion.[c]

2When a country is rebellious, it has many rulers,
but a man of understanding and knowledge maintains order.

3A ruler[y] who oppresses the poor
is like a driving rain that leaves no crops.

4Those who forsake the law praise the wicked,
but those who keep the law resist them.

5Evil men do not understand justice,
but those who seek the LORD understand it fully.

6Better a poor man whose walk is blameless
than a rich man whose ways are perverse.[d]

7He who keeps the law is a discerning son,
but a companion of gluttons disgraces his father.[e]

8He who increases his wealth by exorbitant interest[f]
amasses it for another,[g] who will be kind to the poor.[h]

9If anyone turns a deaf ear to the law,
even his prayers are detestable.[i]

10He who leads the upright along an evil path
will fall into his own trap,[j]
but the blameless will receive a good inheritance.

11A rich man may be wise in his own eyes,
but a poor man who has discernment sees through him.

12When the righteous triumph, there is great elation;[k]
but when the wicked rise to power, men go into hiding.[l]

13He who conceals his sins[m] does not prosper,
but whoever confesses and renounces them finds mercy.[n]

14Blessed is the man who always fears the LORD,
but he who hardens his heart falls into trouble.

15Like a roaring lion or a charging bear
is a wicked man ruling over a helpless people.

16A tyrannical ruler lacks judgment,
but he who hates ill-gotten gain will enjoy a long life.

17A man tormented by the guilt of murder
will be a fugitive[o] till death;
let no one support him.

18He whose walk is blameless is kept safe,
but he whose ways are perverse will suddenly fall.[p]

19He who works his land will have abundant food,
but the one who chases fantasies will have his fill of poverty.[q]

20A faithful man will be richly blessed,
but one eager to get rich will not go unpunished.[r]

21To show partiality is not good[s] —
yet a man will do wrong for a piece of bread.[t]

22A stingy man is eager to get rich
and is unaware that poverty awaits him.[u]

23He who rebukes a man will in the end gain more favor
than he who has a flattering tongue.[v]

24He who robs his father or mother[w]
and says, "It's not wrong"—
he is partner to him who destroys.[x]

25A greedy man stirs up dissension,
but he who trusts in the LORD[y] will prosper.

28:1
[a]2Ki 7:7
[b]Lev 26:17;
Ps 53:5
[c]Ps 138:3

28:6
[d]Pr 19:1

28:7
[e]Pr 23:19-21

28:8
[f]Ex 18:21
[g]Job 27:17;
Pr 13:22
[h]Ps 112:9;
Pr 14:31;
Lk 14:12-14

28:9
[i]Ps 66:18;
109:7;
Pr 15:8;
Isa 1:13

28:10
[j]Pr 26:27

28:12
[k]2Ki 11:20
[l]Pr 11:10;
29:2

28:13
[m]Job 31:33
[n]Ps 32:1-5;
1Jn 1:9

28:17
[o]Ge 9:6

28:18
[p]Pr 10:9

28:19
[q]Pr 12:11

28:20
[r]ver 22;
Pr 10:6;
1Ti 6:9

28:21
[s]Pr 18:5
[t]Eze 13:19

28:22
[u]ver 20;
Pr 23:6

28:23
[v]Pr 27:5-6

28:24
[w]Pr 19:26
[x]Pr 18:9

28:25
[y]Pr 29:25

y3 Or *A poor man*

26He who trusts in himself is a fool,[a]
    but he who walks in wisdom is
        kept safe.

27He who gives to the poor will lack
        nothing,[b]
    but he who closes his eyes to them
        receives many curses.

28When the wicked rise to power,
        people go into hiding;[c]
    but when the wicked perish, the
        righteous thrive.

Rulers and authority.

29 A man who remains stiff-
    necked after many rebukes
    will suddenly be
        destroyed—without remedy.[d]

2When the righteous thrive, the
        people rejoice;[e]
    when the wicked rule, the people
        groan.[f]

3A man who loves wisdom brings joy
        to his father,[g]
    but a companion of prostitutes
        squanders his wealth.[h]

4By justice a king gives a country
        stability,[i]
    but one who is greedy for bribes
        tears it down.

5Whoever flatters his neighbor
    is spreading a net for his feet.

6An evil man is snared by his own
        sin,[j]
    but a righteous one can sing and
        be glad.

7The righteous care about justice for
        the poor,[k]
    but the wicked have no such
        concern.

8Mockers stir up a city,
    but wise men turn away anger.[l]

9If a wise man goes to court with a fool,
    the fool rages and scoffs, and there
        is no peace.

10Bloodthirsty men hate a man of
        integrity

and seek to kill the upright.[m]

11A fool gives full vent to his anger,
    but a wise man keeps himself
        under control.[n]

12If a ruler listens to lies,
    all his officials become wicked.

13The poor man and the oppressor
        have this in common:
    The Lord gives sight to the eyes of
        both.[o]

14If a king judges the poor with
        fairness,
    his throne will always be secure.[p]

15The rod of correction imparts wisdom,
    but a child left to himself disgraces
        his mother.[q]

16When the wicked thrive, so does sin,
    but the righteous will see their
        downfall.[r]

17Discipline your son, and he will give
        you peace;
    he will bring delight to your soul.[s]

18Where there is no revelation, the
        people cast off restraint;
    but blessed is he who keeps the
        law.[t]

19A servant cannot be corrected by
        mere words;
    though he understands, he will not
        respond.

20Do you see a man who speaks in
        haste?
    There is more hope for a fool than
        for him.[u]

21If a man pampers his servant from
        youth,
    he will bring grief[z] in the end.

22An angry man stirs up dissension,
    and a hot-tempered one commits
        many sins.[v]

23A man's pride brings him low,
    but a man of lowly spirit gains
        honor.[w]

28:26
[a]Ps 4:5;
Pr 3:5
28:27
[b]Dt 15:7;
24:19;
Pr 19:17; 22:9
28:28
[c]ver 12
29:1
[d]2Ch 36:16;
Pr 6:15
29:2
[e]Est 8:15
[f]Pr 28:12
29:3
[g]Pr 10:1
[h]Pr 5:8-10;
Lk 15:11-32
29:4
[i]Pr 8:15-16
29:6
[j]Ecc 9:12
29:7
[k]Job 29:16;
Ps 41:1;
Pr 31:8-9
29:8
[l]Pr 11:11;
16:14
29:10
[m]1Jn 3:12
29:11
[n]Pr 12:16;
19:11
29:13
[o]Pr 22:2;
Mt 5:45
29:14
[p]Ps 72:1-5;
Pr 16:12
29:15
[q]Pr 10:1;
13:24;
17:21,25
29:16
[r]Ps 37:35-36;
58:10; 91:8;
92:11
29:17
[s]ver 15;
Pr 10:1
29:18
[t]Ps 1:1-2;
119:1-2;
Jn 13:17
29:20
[u]Pr 26:12;
Jas 1:19
29:22
[v]Pr 14:17;
15:18; 26:21
29:23
[w]Pr 11:2;
15:33; 16:18;
Isa 66:2;
Mt 23:12

[z]21 The meaning of the Hebrew for this word is
uncertain.

24The accomplice of a thief is his own
  enemy;
  he is put under oath and dare not
    testify.*a*

25Fear of man will prove to be a snare,
  but whoever trusts in the LORD *b* is
    kept safe.

26Many seek an audience with a ruler,*c*
  but it is from the LORD that man
    gets justice.

27The righteous detest the dishonest;
  the wicked detest the upright.*d*

Sayings of Agur.

30 The sayings of Agur son of
  Jakeh—an oracle *a* :

This man declared to Ithiel,
  to Ithiel and to Ucal:*b*

2"I am the most ignorant of men;
  I do not have a man's
    understanding.
3I have not learned wisdom,
  nor have I knowledge of the Holy
    One.*e*
4Who has gone up *f* to heaven and
    come down?
  Who has gathered up the wind in
    the hollow*g* of his hands?
  Who has wrapped up the waters *h* in
    his cloak?*i*
  Who has established all the ends of
    the earth?
  What is his name,*j* and the name of
    his son?
  Tell me if you know!

5"Every word of God is flawless; *k*
  he is a shield *l* to those who take
    refuge in him.
6Do not add *m* to his words,
  or he will rebuke you and prove
    you a liar.

7"Two things I ask of you, O LORD;
  do not refuse me before I die:
8Keep falsehood and lies far from me;
  give me neither poverty nor
    riches,
  but give me only my daily bread. *n*

9Otherwise, I may have too much and
    disown*o* you
  and say, 'Who is the LORD?'*p*
Or I may become poor and steal,
  and so dishonor the name of my
    God. *q*

10"Do not slander a servant to his
    master,
  or he will curse you, and you will
    pay for it.

11"There are those who curse their
    fathers
  and do not bless their mothers; *r*
12those who are pure in their own
    eyes*s*
  and yet are not cleansed of their
    filth;*t*
13those whose eyes are ever so
    haughty,*u*
  whose glances are so disdainful;
14those whose teeth*v* are swords
  and whose jaws are set with
    knives *w*
to devour*x* the poor*y* from the earth,
  the needy from among mankind.*z*

15"The leech has two daughters.
  'Give! Give!' they cry.

"There are three things that are
    never satisfied,*a*
  four that never say, 'Enough!':
16the grave,*c b* the barren womb,
  land, which is never satisfied with
    water,
  and fire, which never says,
    'Enough!'

17"The eye that mocks*c* a father,
  that scorns obedience to a mother,
will be pecked out by the ravens of
    the valley,
  will be eaten by the vultures. *d*

18"There are three things that are too
    amazing for me,
  four that I do not understand:

Cross-references

29:24
*a*Lev 5:1
29:25
*b*Pr 28:25
29:26
*c*Pr 19:6
29:27
*d*ver 10
30:3
*e*Pr 9:10
30:4
*f*Ps 24:1-2;
Jn 3:13;
Eph 4:7-10
*g*Ps 104:3;
Isa 40:12
*h*Job 26:8;
38:8-9
*i*Ge 1:2
*j*Rev 19:12
30:5
*k*Ps 12:6;
18:30
*l*Ge 15:1;
Ps 84:11
30:6
*m*Dt 4:2;
12:32;
Rev 22:18
30:8
*n*Mt 6:11
30:9
*o*Jos 24:27;
Isa 1:4; 59:13
*p*Dt 6:12;
8:10-14;
Hos 13:6
*q*Dt 8:12
30:11
*r*Pr 20:20
30:12
*s*Pr 16:2;
Lk 18:11
*t*Jer 2:23,35
30:13
*u*2Sa 22:28;
Job 41:34;
Ps 131:1;
Pr 6:17
30:14
*v*Job 4:11;
29:17;
Ps 3:7
*w*Ps 57:4
*x*Job 24:9;
Ps 14:4
*y*Am 8:4;
Mic 2:2
*z*Job 19:22
30:15
*a*Pr 27:20
30:16
*b*Pr 27:20;
Isa 5:14;
14:9,11;
Hab 2:5

30:17*c*Dt 21:18-21; Pr 23:22 *d*Job 15:23

a *1* Or *Jakeh of Massa*   b *1* Masoretic Text; with a
different word division of the Hebrew *declared, "I am
weary, O God; / I am weary, O God, and faint.*
c *16* Hebrew *Sheol*

19the way of an eagle in the sky,
the way of a snake on a rock,
the way of a ship on the high seas,
and the way of a man with a maiden.

20"This is the way of an adulteress:
She eats and wipes her mouth
and says, 'I've done nothing wrong.'[a]

21"Under three things the earth trembles,
under four it cannot bear up:
22a servant who becomes king,[b]
a fool who is full of food,
23an unloved woman who is married,
and a maidservant who displaces her mistress.

24"Four things on earth are small,
yet they are extremely wise:
25Ants are creatures of little strength,
yet they store up their food in the summer;[c]
26coneys[d] [d] are creatures of little power,
yet they make their home in the crags;
27locusts[e] have no king,
yet they advance together in ranks;
28a lizard can be caught with the hand,
yet it is found in kings' palaces.

29"There are three things that are stately in their stride,
four that move with stately bearing:
30a lion, mighty among beasts,
who retreats before nothing;
31a strutting rooster, a he-goat,
and a king with his army around him.[e]

32"If you have played the fool and exalted yourself,
or if you have planned evil,
clap your hand over your mouth![f]
33For as churning the milk produces butter,
and as twisting the nose produces blood,
so stirring up anger produces strife."

30:20 [a]Pr 5:6
30:22 [b]Pr 19:10; 29:2
30:25 [c]Pr 6:6-8
30:26 [d]Ps 104:18
30:27 [e]Ex 10:4
30:32 [f]Job 21:5; 29:9
31:1 [g]Pr 22:17
31:2 [h]Jdg 11:30; Isa 49:15
31:3 [i]Dt 17:17; 1Ki 11:3; Ne 13:26; Pr 5:1-14
31:4 [j]Pr 20:1; Ecc 10:16-17; Isa 5:22
31:5 [k]1Ki 16:9 [l]Pr 16:12; Hos 4:11
31:6 [m]Ge 14:18
31:7 [n]Est 1:10
31:8 [o]1Sa 19:4; Job 29:12-17
31:9 [p]Lev 19:15; Dt 1:16; Pr 24:23; 29:7; Isa 1:17; Jer 22:16
31:10 [q]Ru 3:11; Pr 12:4; 18:22 [r]Pr 8:35; 19:14
31:11 [s]Ge 2:18 [t]Pr 12:4
31:13 [u]1Ti 2:9-10

Sayings of King Lemuel.

31 The sayings[g] of King Lemuel—
an oracle[f] his mother taught him:

2"O my son, O son of my womb,
O son of my vows,[g] [h]
3do not spend your strength on women,
your vigor on those who ruin kings.[i]

4"It is not for kings, O Lemuel—
not for kings to drink wine,[j]
not for rulers to crave beer,
5lest they drink[k] and forget what the law decrees,[l]
and deprive all the oppressed of their rights.
6Give beer to those who are perishing,
wine[m] to those who are in anguish;
7let them drink[n] and forget their poverty
and remember their misery no more.

8"Speak[o] up for those who cannot speak for themselves,
for the rights of all who are destitute.
9Speak up and judge fairly;
defend the rights of the poor and needy."[p]

Description of a wife of noble character.

10[h]A wife of noble character[q] who can find?[r]
She is worth far more than rubies.
11Her husband[s] has full confidence in her
and lacks nothing of value.[t]
12She brings him good, not harm,
all the days of her life.
13She selects wool and flax
and works with eager hands.[u]
14She is like the merchant ships,
bringing her food from afar.

[d]*26* That is, the hyrax or rock badger [e]*31* Or *king secure against revolt* [f]*1* Or *of Lemuel king of Massa, which* [g]*2* Or */ the answer to my prayers* [h]*10* Verses 10-31 are an acrostic, each verse beginning with a successive letter of the Hebrew alphabet.

¹⁵She gets up while it is still dark;
    she provides food for her family
    and portions for her servant girls.
¹⁶She considers a field and buys it;
    out of her earnings she plants a
    vineyard.
¹⁷She sets about her work vigorously;
    her arms are strong for her tasks.
¹⁸She sees that her trading is profitable,
    and her lamp does not go out at
    night.
¹⁹In her hand she holds the distaff
    and grasps the spindle with her
    fingers.
²⁰She opens her arms to the poor
    and extends her hands to the
    needy.[a]
²¹When it snows, she has no fear for
    her household;
    for all of them are clothed in scarlet.
²²She makes coverings for her bed;
    she is clothed in fine linen and
    purple.
²³Her husband is respected at the city
    gate,
    where he takes his seat among the
    elders[b] of the land.

31:20
[a]Dt 15:11;
Eph 4:28;
Heb 13:16

31:23
[b]Ex 3:16;
Ru 4:1,11;
Pr 12:4

31:26
[c]Pr 10:31

31:31
[d]Pr 11:16

²⁴She makes linen garments and sells
    them,
    and supplies the merchants with
    sashes.
²⁵She is clothed with strength and
    dignity;
    she can laugh at the days to come.
²⁶She speaks with wisdom,
    and faithful instruction is on her
    tongue.[c]
²⁷She watches over the affairs of her
    household
    and does not eat the bread of
    idleness.
²⁸Her children arise and call her
    blessed;
    her husband also, and he praises
    her:
²⁹"Many women do noble things,
    but you surpass them all."
³⁰Charm is deceptive, and beauty is
    fleeting;
    but a woman who fears the LORD is
    to be praised.
³¹Give her the reward she has earned,
    and let her works bring her
    praise[d] at the city gate.

ℐ NDEX OF ℕ AMES

You can find *A RAINBOW OF HOPE*
and THE RAINBOW STUDY BIBLE
wherever fine books are sold.